FROM POVERTY TO PROSPERITY
THE TRUTH ABOUT THE WEALTH OF GOD'S LOVE

Nikia Anderson

From Poverty to Prosperity
The Truth About the Wealth of God's Love

Copyright © 2024 by Nikia Anderson

All rights reserved. This book or any portion thereof may not be reproduced or used in any manner whatsoever without the express written consent of the publisher except for the use of brief quotations in articles and reviews.

Printed in the United States of America

Author: Nikia Anderson

ISBN: 979-8-9903974-7-7

Library of Congress Control Number: 2024915387

Edited & Published by: Ahvision Publishing
www.ahvisionpublishing.com

TABLE OF CONTENTS

PREFACE: Living This Thing Called Life	7
CHAPTER 1: What Is Love?	13
CHAPTER 2: People And Their Impact On Your Life	25
CHAPTER 3: "The Change You Are Calling For Starts With Us"	39
CHAPTER 4: Not Allowing The Past To Control Your Future	45
CHAPTER 5: The Kid Who Made It Out Of The Slums	51
MINI STORIES: Slice of Humble Pie / Strength in Faith	65
CHAPTER 6: A Testimony Of God's Presence And Revelation	79
CHAPTER 7: The World We Live In Today	91
CHAPTER 8: Revelation Of The Times	99
CHAPTER 9: What Would You Do For Eternity?	107
CHAPTER 10: The Race For Humanity	113
PHOTOS: Photography By The Author	125
BIBLE REFERENCES: According to the Text	133
ABOUT THE AUTHOR	140

DEDICATION

This book is dedicated to the love of family and to all those who helped shape my life experiences. A special dedication goes to **Gary Louis Booker II**, whose birth into eternity brought Love to a struggling people. Rest in LOVE, my brother, and may your contagious smile be engrained in our hearts and memories forever.

PREFACE
Living This Thing Called Life

Life is a testing journey, no matter where you live or who you are. There are many ups and downs, highs and lows, ins and outs, but regardless of your background or history, if you get to live it, life is truly a blessing. They say that all people are created equal, which is a statement I fully agree with, but not everyone is born into equal circumstances. This would be a more accurate statement. Some are born into the world being heirs of wealth, while others are born into extreme poverty. Both are given a chance at this thing we call life. The fundamental principle of life at its very essence is love! Some are born into love, while others search their entire lives and come up short.

From carrying buckets of water from a neighbor's house at the age of five so that we would have clean water to drink to having to make the most difficult phone call a son could ever make to his mother, life has had its toll on challenging the principles that I bring to you through my writings. Yes, I was the one to tell my mother that she had lost her baby boy in a tragic car accident just three weeks before he would have graduated college. Through many losses over the years, including a ton of relationships, some of which I destroyed in my selfish acts, true love somehow found a way to plant itself in the shriveled soils of my fragmented heart.

See, a man, in his immaturity, will blame everyone for his problems except for the one who caused them. The long sleepless nights spent in worry, the battles in and out of the court systems, the time wasted while not being able to see my kids, the tormented belief that I could figure it out on my own just before going through horrible breakups with the people who I thought loved me, and the numerous judgments that I passed along to others has taught me the ability to overcome the mistakes in this life in order to receive the promise of peace. This promise is given to all who choose to live in righteousness. It was not until having all these experiences and being changed by them that I realized the value of love and true peace.

As I have traveled all over this world and spent time with diverse types of people, I have experienced these things at their core. Each place has been different, along with their perspectives on life. However, there is one thing that has been consistent throughout all the journeys. I have found my heart crying out to the ones I have met on multiple occasions. I have even shared moments of tears with many people, according to the joy and fullness of my heart. This is one of the letters I wrote to my family back home during one of those trips:

Well, I have a confession to make. I have had the happiest, healthiest cries after my last three classes here recently. Joy has filled my heart, and I have been overcome by emotions. I guess it is safe to say that my heart is vested in what I believe in.

I am thankful for the people I have met. He has shown me more of His Love through those whom I have had an opportunity to touch. I just hope I have shown them the image. He would be proud of my character and not just of my words.

Thanks be to the Father above for these journeys! They have really helped me to see the importance of family and keeping God above all things. I also want to thank all the family for your love and support throughout my time away from you! Without you, this would be extremely difficult. Please continue to pray for me as I continue to do the same for you.

These are some of the messages that were sent to me by some of the people who I had the opportunity to encounter on those trips abroad:

From: Isaac - *"Thank you for your guidance, strength, wisdom, and thank you for being a real human. I am forever indebted to you, sir! You have brought meaning in a different way. You are a man of Allah!"* – **Isaac**

From: June - *"Hi, Nik. Safe travel for you! I could not say this earlier in class because I didn't want to get too emotional, and I didn't want to use up the remaining time left. Thank you for everything! You're a one-of-a-kind trainer. You're the friendliest and most approachable trainer I've ever met. May God continue to bless you and your family.*

To be honest, I don't know if God intended you to be our trainer, but please do include me in your prayers. I am a backslidden Christian. My family disowned me. I have so much hatred towards my mom because she said the most hurtful words to me. I am living alone. I stopped praying and stopped attending Church. I have literally become depressed three times this year and had become suicidal. If it wasn't for a few concerned friends, I wouldn't be alive today.

I am mad at God for the things that have happened to my life. I blame Him for what's happened between my mom and me. I hope this isn't too much to ask for, but please do pray for me. I really appreciate your advice. When you reminded me about love being able to cover a multitude of sins, it struck me really hard and made me realize that I don't love my mom because I keep resenting her. I have not grown in love.

One more prayer request is that there will be no hatred nor bitterness among our group. There have been internal issues. I also had an argument with another learner a few days ago. Even though I apologized, he has a heart of stone. I apologized several times thru Messenger. No reply. Then he blocked me. It can be discouraging to be in a team where we have hard feelings towards one another. Please pray for our team, for me, and for us not to stay bitter.

I know this is a long message, but I believe things happen for a reason. Continue to share the light of Jesus to remind those lukewarm Christians and backslidden Christians of Jesus' love. Moreover, the unbelievers being able to see Jesus in you. Thank you so much, Nik. You're one of the best trainers ever! I hope you've enjoyed your stay with us. The things you share will be forever kept in our hearts and thank you for the spiritual advice. I thank God for sending you. To be honest, you're a great inspiration and an influencer. I am so inspired by your training, and I can indeed see your life testimony. I've learned so much from you. You will never be forgotten! Among all the training I had been through before, this has been the most emotional. To some, you're an answered prayer." – **June**

From: Gabby - *"Hey Nik! I couldn't thank you enough for everything yesterday. We didn't have much time, but I'm so thankful that I met you. They say God's timing is perfect, and I believe in that. You taught me so much and every piece of advice, every lesson, everything you taught me, I will keep it in mind and cherish it. You are a great person! May God bless you and your family always! Thank you! Hope to see you soon!"* – **Gabby**

From: Marco - *"Happy trip, my brother...I will treasure every day that you shared your knowledge with us and also some of the advice you gave me from a father-to-father perspective. Keep in touch...and if you come back, let me know. I thank you from the bottom of my heart...God bless you and your family!"* – **Marco**

I authored this book as an example of all these concepts I mentioned above in hopes that it would give you the courage to fight through the valleys of life and come into the enjoyment of the mountaintops of love. Let me be clear: while this book contains a multitude of things that everyone would benefit from, it is not going to be for everyone. This book is filled with a lot of stories, perspectives, methods, and ideas that spark change and growth, but there are a lot of people in the world today who fear change and resort to living in comfort. Some will read the first few pages and call it quits, while others will read halfway through and say to themselves, this is ludicrous, but I bring you the truth according to the love I have for each one of you! You will also find many quotes, statements, mini-stories, pictures, poems, scriptures, and tons of references throughout my writings to help you connect with the experience that lies within this body of works.

Do yourself the honor of looking up the references provided, as they will really enhance your experience throughout reading this book. Take the time to read them alongside the messages they correspond with. I wrote in this manner with the intent that you would be able to learn and grow in understanding and knowledge, not from my perspective only, but that you would learn from applying your own perspective as well. If you are the type of reader who loves to read fast, I would suggest that after you read it through the first time, go back and read it slowly with the purpose of applying the concepts that you have read about. Not to spill any of the goodness of this book, but you will find a lot about pain, growth, change, and love throughout this journey.

Ideally, the reader would read a few pages per day to allow for time to apply the concepts within. These principles all relate to how a kid without running water could make it out of those conditions and survive in a world that seemed to be against him from the beginning of his time of memory. In all his wrongs and in all of his pain, he found what it means to live life on purpose.

For those who read it to its end, I hope that you, too, can find the true love in life that is waiting for you. Through my struggles and pain, I hope that you will find joy, laughter, and peace in your own life. This book is written as a tribute to you through all of your seeking of love and serves as a guide of understanding through all things.

> *"Don't allow this world or materialistic things to define you. You can be who you are and still be authentic. Only YOU can define YOU."*

CHAPTER I

What Is Love?

"Be kind and compassionate to one another, forgiving each other, just as in Christ God forgave you."
(Ephesians 4:32, NIV)

CHAPTER 1
What Is LOVE?

In this world, there is good, and there is evil. You always have a choice, and when you make the choice to do that which is righteous, the world comes at you a lot easier. You will eliminate a lot of the stress and pressures that come along with making the wrong choices. You begin to live by faith and with genuine LOVE. You also begin to see the choices in this world that are contrary to that which is good. You cannot un-see what has been seen. It is through these choices that you start to find your true LOVE and happiness.

There is a difference between looking happy and being happy. When you are genuinely happy, nothing can come between you and your happiness. They say that happiness is where the heart is, so make the choice of allowing LOVE to take its rightful place and reside over your heart. The reality is this: we have all made bad choices in our past, and we should not be ashamed of the ones that we have made. Once you choose to open your eyes to the hatred the world wants us to have for one another, you can never close them to the truth. LOVE and hatred then become a choice that clearly is within the perspective of those who see it. Learn to trust in yourself and start making better choices. This will show you a different view of the world and what is important in life.

There then comes a point in your life where you must examine the situations that surround you. The reality is a lot of people are not healed from their previous situations. Those very issues that they are not healed from will manifest themselves in their present environment. Once doubt, the enemy of forward progression, sets in, there is almost nothing you can do to overcome it other than helping them to realize it. If they take heed and responsibility for the impact their past is having on them, then they will begin to understand where the problems lie. The question becomes, will they commit to loving themselves enough to move forward on the path to new opportunities, or will they allow their past to reside within their present?

People are temporary, LOVE is permanent.

LOVE hurts! In order to genuinely LOVE others, you must LOVE them more than you LOVE yourself. You must be willing to LOVE them enough to see yourself in them. This will change how you view and treat others. You cannot be selfish and LOVE people the way they should be LOVED at the same time. True LOVE requires sacrifice. Don't get my words twisted; I never said to lose yourself in LOVING others because people will fully test the depths of your LOVE if you allow them. However, there is no selfishness in true LOVE.

LOVE requires an understanding of how to LOVE others, and you must be deeply rooted in your self-LOVE and fully aware of who you are in order to put yourself aside to LOVE others. A huge part of LOVE requires service. Service implies that you must have the ability to demonstrate the actions of helping others. So, if you want to achieve a fruitful, LOVE-filled life, learn how to be comfortable enough with yourself that you can put self-LOVE/selfishness aside long enough to serve others. This is the embodiment of true LOVE.

"They must have a lot of layers," people often say, but people with a lot of layers LOVE the hardest. Others who are not used to that type of LOVE take advantage of people with a lot of layers, which causes them to go into a shell and abandon the loving spirit they have been giving freely. It's extremely hard to get them out of that state of mind once they have experienced the brokenness that stems from having their LOVE taken for granted. Once their trust is broken, it requires a lot of truth, honesty, and actions of loyalty to open them back up. It also takes a lot of "looking in the mirror" on their behalf, and it requires them to face the hurt that has become a part of their personality. This is the beginning of the healing process.

The pain that you inflict onto others will manifest itself through your own life if you don't learn how to face the actions that led to the hurt.

Energy can put you in places you have never been before, just like the force of a hurricane. It can push aside your problems, similar to waves hitting the seashore. The Energy you put out is the same energy you will receive. Some of us allow negative energy to push us to the point of earthquakes, while others promote energy that moves like the direction of the winds that provide a cool breeze on a summer evening. If you could choose which energy you put out into the world, which kind would it be? Now, look in the mirror and act on the energy you want to see!

Be strong, be patient, and know that God can overcome all hurt. God is a Healer in the midst of hurt.

We have it all wrong; we have been LOVING others through the eyes of man. God wants us to view LOVE through His eyes! Just remember, there are some who are against God, and His enemies have already fallen from His grace. Don't let them take you with them! The enemy gets a victory every time you allow circumstances or situations to impact your character in a negative way. That is their goal, and now that you know their game, it should change the way you play. Remember, LOVE will forever reign over hate, just as life prevails over death. It's up to us to choose!

Learn to LOVE like God. God's LOVE is not based on what someone does to you or how they treat you. That's called conditional LOVE, not Agape LOVE. Agape is LOVE without condition, the highest form of LOVE, without fail, and it is everlasting. LOVE people enough to see beyond the outer shell, which no one has the ability to choose, and learn to see yourself in others. Find genuine good/appreciation in everyone, even in troubled times.

You cannot learn God's will just by looking at history. History is what people were doing, not what God wanted them to do. John the Baptist was dead when the church was invented, just like David never saw the temple. There can be benefits to conflict. You will have conflicts; the question is, will you put aside your selfishness and find the LOVE to resolve them? Do you know why no one has been able to overcome the issues they are facing? It's because no one has prayed for them and shown them the LOVE of God. The LOVE of God is what will overcome those issues and you have that very same LOVE flowing within you.

Learn to say what is wrong and do not play psychological games with people. If you have a problem with someone, you take it to them and them alone. If they do not hear you, take the opportunity to release your negative energy and be willing to find peace. Learn to apologize, even when you feel as though others do not deserve it. Your apology is not for them, it is for you to start the process of moving forward. By releasing the negative energy associated with the situation, you can start the journey toward receiving peace in your heart. By not allowing the stain of bad emotions to overpower you and change your character, you are able to strengthen the LOVE within your heart, allowing room for healthy energy. It is peace that brings about joy. Joy is one of the many things that is achieved with Agape LOVE!

Show people that you care enough by being honest with them. Don't pacify them by giving falsehoods or misleading them about their behaviors. Let me be honest with you: I have been guilty of doing this in the past. My fear was that I would hurt someone's feelings or make them feel bad, but I failed to consider the impact I had on people by not being upfront and honest with them. Don't get my words twisted. I did not say for you to start confronting people with strong words and an attitude. There must be a method to how you talk to people. Getting into a confrontation would be missing the whole point of showing people that you care for them. Gentleness and genuineness must be a part of this conversation and it must come from a place of compassion and understanding. I had to learn the hard way to not be afraid of telling people when they are making mistakes. Not only do we waste their time, but we also create doubt in our character by assuming they appreciate good words as opposed to the words of truth.

Ultimately, some people will take your honesty the wrong way, but just know that it comes from a place of caring LOVE. I've learned that it's the people who care about you that want to see you do better. How can you get better if no one is criticizing you? You would always think you are doing everything right if no one ever provided you with their observations, and we can all use help in some areas of improvement. Until you learn to confront and resolve barriers, you will not grow.

Growth scares people who are afraid of change. LOVE them anyway. Sometimes, a person is so hurt that you must LOVE them from a distance and allow them to learn how to LOVE themselves. Remember, it usually has nothing to do with you at all. Learn to LOVE them for who they are, and this does not always mean that you will be present in their life.

You must be willing to accept people for who they are. LOVE is about acceptance. As people, we have to get to the point where we can be comfortable with agreeing to disagree—"I respect and appreciate your honesty, and I LOVE you more because of it." We can always respect genuineness and honesty. There comes a time in life when you learn to LOVE and accept people for who they are. Just know that regardless, you will always be LOVED the way you should be LOVED by the LOVE Giver, who so LOVED the world that He gave us the greatest gift you and I could ever receive. You are now three times redeemed from the hatred of the enemy, so do not allow the enemy's ways to keep you from the LOVE of The Creator. He created you and I to do the work of good/righteousness. Reclaim your independence through Him and remove your dependence on the works of the adversary. We are all of One Interdependence of LOVE, which glorifies the LOVE Giver!

READ | Ephesians 4:32

Independence stems from a state of dependence, and both are essential steps necessary to achieve interdependence.

MINI-STORY: A Story of Love

A few years back, my son and I were at the park going for a light jog when we came across an elderly couple walking on the trail. The elderly gentleman was holding an umbrella over the head of his wife with disabilities, who was trying her best to walk along with her cane. It was the beginning of summer in Arkansas, and it was a little after noontime. On this scorching summer afternoon, as they walked, she would take a break, and her husband would stop to make sure she was ok. As we passed them, we waved, and I greeted them.

When we came back, we saw them again. Something told me to speak to the man, so I introduced myself and I simply thanked him for showing his LOVE for his wife. I went on to explain to him how he was an inspiration of LOVE. "It's rare to find true LOVE in this world these days!" I said. The man told us his name and how he used to exercise a lot in his former years. He stated that his wife just LOVED being around him. I was taken aback by this because she suffered through so much pain just to show her husband that she LOVED him and supported what he LOVED to do. He asked my son what his name was and had him spell it for him. He proceeded to tell him that his dad, who was overwhelmed with tears at this point, was a healthy man and that he put in a lot of hard work to look as good as he did. He went on to tell my son and me that practice and dedication are the two most important things to accomplish what you want in life.

As we walked away, my son asked me why I cried. I told him, "Because LOVE, true LOVE, is so hard to find these days, and when you do, it will withstand the test of time." This story was proof to me that I had not come as far as I did for nothing. We all deserve a better LOVE. This type of LOVE is the LOVE that will endure all things and grow over time. The LOVE I am referring to is a LOVE that is built on honesty, trust, and loyalty. This is the same type of LOVE that I show my kids because of the LOVE I have from The Father, who LOVES us so much. When I think about the people I LOVE, all I can do is cry tears of joy about all the good I see in them. Even when they do not listen to me, I still LOVE them so much! I would give them the world according to my LOVE because they deserve it.

So, I am back to the question: what is LOVE? As my late brother would do to those who he met in his short twenty-one years on this earth, showing LOVE is about LOVING people regardless of what they do to you or say about you. LOVE is something that is given freely without the expectation that you are gaining anything from it. Loving others is about giving according to the greatness within your heart because you have been given LOVE through the freedom of life.

To this day, I still remember the day my brother passed on from this life so vividly. It is as though it just happened yesterday. The LOVE we shared was more than just the LOVE that you would expect of brothers. He was more like a son to me. As I stood looking at his lifeless body lying on a gurney, I realized that peace and tranquility were all over his face. He had that slight smile that we all had become so familiar with seeing on him. This gave me strength to receive calmness in my spirit in such a dreadful moment. It looked as though he was lying there sleeping, as he would do after a long day's work. I wanted to walk over to him and slap him jokingly, as I would often do if I found him asleep, and yell out to him, "WAKE UP, DUDE!"

It was at this moment that I remembered hearing the first "I LOVE you" words from many of our family members who had arrived at the funeral home. See, this was one of the first times that I could ever remember our family using those words. LOVE was something that was implied but rarely spoken about in our family. Little did I know this moment of catastrophic loss and dire pain would change that forever. It was these moments that changed our family eternally! We realized that, as human beings, we never know when our time is coming to leave this earth and life is too short to live it in regret. Through these series of events, we learned that LOVE is something that we are obliged to give away always, and it should always be properly conveyed, as opposed to just implied. So, what is the best example of this LOVE that I speak about? GOD is the answer!

READ
John 3:16
1 John 4:7-21

Trust the path you are on. You may not understand everything, but remember, nothing happens without reason. It's all a part of the plan and the path for your purpose, leading you to have trust in Him.

CHAPTER II

People And Their Impact On Your Life

"Or do you show contempt for the riches of his kindness, forbearance and patience, not realizing that God's kindness is intended to lead you to repentance?"
(Romans 2:4, NIV)

CHAPTER 2
People and Their Impact on Your Life

We often give people all our LOVE, thinking that their hearts are exactly the same as ours. The reality is some people are looking to rob our hearts of all the goodness they possess. We tend to hold on to the hope that everyone is just like us and that if they are not, they will eventually change and stop drinking from our cup of goodness. In the end, we finally realize that we have allowed our cups to be emptied by the drinkers. We then realize that our cups need a refill, while all along, we act oblivious to the fact that we are seeing the cups get lower and lower.

This ideology is what gets us into a lot of the situations we face in life. What we must understand is that a great heart also must come with discernment. Just because you have a big heart does not mean that you put it out into the world to be devoured like a steak from Ruth's Chris. A divine HEART is a HEART that is also protected. Don't allow your heart to be drained of the blood of salvation because of your lack of discernment and your inability to realize that the cup comes with a lid. Stay vigilant! LOVE hard and protect your heart.

People with big hearts must stop sharing their hearts with the people who only take from your goodness. Give love freely to those who are willing to receive it and not take advantage of it. Takers will continue to take because it is what they are good at. So, only give to those who show they deserve it. The reality is some people will go looking for reasons to push themselves away from you. Let them! Your growth will cause you to lose people/things.

You are in a season of growth, and you must understand that some things are not meant to continue into this season.

Even the trees lose their leaves in the fall, and only the people/things that are necessary will continue with you on your journey. Don't allow your growth to be stunted by those who are too blind to see your vision. During your growth season, you will need people in your corner to support you. If they cannot support you in being better, especially when you are going through life and trying to do better, then they do not genuinely LOVE you the way they should LOVE you. Remember, God would want to see you doing better, and if people cannot support you in doing so, they are not heaven-sent.

Be cautious of those whom you share your problems with. Not every listening ear is there to help you with solutions, most are there to ensure you continue your struggles. If you continue to indulge with those who tend to entertain filth, you are bound to eventually get dirty yourself. Remember, misery loves company.

    Some of us put ourselves through hell on earth with all the situations we get into as a result of having the wrong people around us. I think we all know of these people/situations that I speak of. These are the very situations/people that we knew we needed to remove ourselves from, but having the fortitude to do so was a different story. These types of people are the result of a lot of the issues we are facing right now in this world. I would suggest we all find The Lord. We must not allow the adversary to trick us into thinking that he can win! Clarity comes when we start to recognize the environment around us, along with the situations we are putting ourselves in.

    The moment you feel yourself being dragged down the wrong roads, you have a duty to act. By not doing so, you are allowing yourself to become a worker for the enemy. It's time to show the LOVE that you should show for yourself by doing something for "You." Seek more of His LOVE. You are worthy of giving yourself a chance by seeking Him.

This world is full of people who are trying to be someone/something they are not. This is because they are not happy with who they are. They are always hoping and wishing for other people's downfall. This becomes a cancer to others around them, and if they let it, it will consume them. It's OK to be you. "The only competition I have is ME; therefore, I'm comfortable in my own skin. I see no competition, only myself."

They say that there is a ravenous wolf on the prowl amongst mortal men. He's seeking those whom he may devour. The enemy has a hold on people. He's been busy doing some of his best work through them. A lot of people are still riding with lies! It is through his fabrications that he keeps so many people from the promises made to them. Remember, the enemy is always looking for a way to win. He's a master of deceit and is constantly trying to play his games with you. He always tries to plant his thoughts in your head. Be conscious of the forces at work in your presence. Awareness gives you the advantage over the enemy. Once you recognize situations that are not conducive to positivity, remove yourself from those surroundings. Elevation requires separation! To reach your new heights, you will need to remove some of the dead weight that is holding you in your current space.

READ
Job 1:6, 2:1
1 John 3:7-10
James 1:15, 2:19, 3:15
Ephesians 2:1-10

These thoughts that the enemy is planting in your head are only tests. The goal is to see how strong your faith is. If your faith is strong, it ends up reminding you how strong and mighty the Lord is. One way to gauge how well you are doing with this is to evaluate how you are feeling in the middle of the storm.

If you can see yourself getting closer to God, then you are strengthening your faith. If you find yourself in doubt about everything, remember it is never too late. It is in this moment that you can change the momentum. This is the trivial moment in which you can turn to Him before it is too late. Consequently, the enemy knows the power of your vision, the very vision that lies within the mind. These visions often manifest themselves in the conversations that we carry on with others. If you want to know what is in a person's field of vision, listen to what they are talking about. What you envision is what you become. All creativity and innovation come from vision. Don't allow others to cloud your visions. If negativity, envy, and malicious thoughts are a routine part of the conversations that you have with people, you may want to consider the impact those interactions are having on your future. It may be time for you to change your audience before those same things become a part of your everyday life. Take time out to look around you to see who is for or against your visions. If the people around you, your inner circle, are always challenging your vision, stop sharing your visions with those individuals. Beware of the vision killers in your life.

You will soon find out that the closer you get to God, the farther away you will get from some people. Weaker spirits will say that you have changed, while others will say it is growth. Either way, they are both talking, but God provides relief from all judgment. Judgment is one of the most deadly diseases amongst the modern human race! The person who says they have not or do not judge others makes themselves out to be a lie. Too many of us cannot recognize our judgments, which becomes a disease to society. Each begins to take judgment into their own hands, thus making themselves righteous in their own ways. Even Yehoshua (Jesus, as Westerners call Him) says, I am The Way, The Truth, The Life, yet we forget His Torah (teachings)! It's up to you to stay focused on listening to Him and not those who put themselves in the judgment seat.

Remember, everything connected to the vine grows, even that which is pruned. The problem is that so many have separated themselves from the vine. What in your life today is causing you to be disconnected? Even with all that is going on around you, The Creator will never cut you off. By faith, we received grace and mercy, which are evident in the fact that He allowed you to open your eyes this morning! Troubles do not last long, and remember, the greater the troubles, the bigger the blessings! Remain faithful and give those battles over to Him. Through those victories, He gains all the Glory! Blessed are those who remain strong through the trials and tribulations. There are people praying for you, even when you do not know it.

Reading and prayer become crucial, and being open to change and humility are also very important in this phase.
Be willing to admit your faults and confess them. Your vision of life determines a lot about your values, expectations, relationships, goals, and priorities. He sees all and knows all, as He is an Omni-Present God. There is no need to hold on to your faults because they have already been forgiven. His hand is always out for us to grab; it is up to us to stop slapping it away.

"Verily, Allâh knows the hidden realities of the heavens and the earth. He knows full well the innermost secret of the minds (of the people)."

The Holy Qur'ân
Al-Fâtir 35:38

READ
Psalms 14:1-6
John 14:6, 15:1-17
Romans 2:4
1 Peter 2:20
Hebrews 12:25-29

Understanding someone else begins when you start to remove self.

Stop allowing others to block your blessings. If you want to be happy, then be happy. If you want to be loved, love yourself. Stop allowing other people to influence or validate your future. It's YOUR future, with or without them. Do not treat people like they are kids. They are adults. Thus, they will do what they want to do regardless, so let them be who they choose to be. They are the ones who must deal with the consequences. Love them for who they are.

READ | 2 Peter 2:10-22

It is extremely hard to listen to a person who will not admit to any wrongdoings whatsoever. Even when they get caught in their lies, they still will not admit any guilt or take responsibility for what part they had in their fabrications. This leads the people around them to do one of two things: either they defend the lies by making it seem like you are the one who created the situation, or they disassociate themselves from the wrongdoings they have experienced with these types of people because they tried to make them part of their problems too. They are forced to defend themselves against the lies by removing any associations with the rhetoric/narrative that was pushed because their character is strong enough not to allow their souls to be taken with them and the darkness that surrounds them.

You wonder why it seems like things are closing in on you. You wonder why people are questioning your moves. You wonder why people around you are dropping left and right. Maybe this is what you intended. Just understand that this is why people are reluctant to rally behind you. It's the depth of your character, and it is very shallow with all the false witnesses that are present in your words. However, then again, fake has been winning over real. Maybe real is the new fake, and vice versa. Maybe honesty is actually a lie, and a lie is actually honesty.

No, on the contrary, being honest with people would accomplish a lot more. We all want to like you; we genuinely do, but you are making it hard for us to trust you with all the talking out of both sides of your mouth. We are seeing these situations play out all around you. The question becomes, who have you sold your soul to, and what do you owe them in return?

These are the same type of people who are quick to holler out "PRAY FOR ME" but will not pray for themselves. It is for this same reason that they feel comfortable asking you for something that they will not give themselves. Stop looking out to the world for help in the tough times and start looking inward for true change. You must first help yourself so that others can help you. Humble yourself just enough to realize that selfishness could be causing most of your issues. "Lord, please protect me from myself."

One of life's biggest struggles is choosing between dwelling on the past or choosing to move forward from it. What I can tell you about this subject is that we know the results of the past. The future is unknown. Don't allow the weight of the past to hold you back from the future that is promised to you. You will become uncomfortable venturing into the land of the unknown, but your future will be written in your own ink. People often allow their past to control them, forgetting that the past does not determine who they are today. Dwelling in the past is a sure way to prevent prosperity in the future. Learn and move forward! Growth is the sign of learning from past experiences. Be Fearless! Growth doesn't happen in the past; it starts now. The choice is yours.

Growth is linear, so be cognizant of circular situations. Lies are circular; the truth is linear. Following the crowd is circular, and standing alone is linear. Push yourself to think beyond the circles in your life.

Take the time to show people that you care for them. Reciprocation is the key to LOVE. People are the most important thing in life. Once they are gone, you cannot get them back, so take the time to give back what they give you. If they cannot give you this, move forward because time is too valuable to waste. The greatest gift you can ever give someone is your time. Make sure that you spend it right because you will never get it back. Think back to your loved ones who have passed away. What would you give to have two minutes of time with them right now? Why should we be allowed more time if we are just going to waste it? Invest your time wisely.

We are living in the times of the strongest faith, but remember, there are two sides to this coin. This is a matter of the perspectives of the World we choose to see. You can choose to see a World of LOVE or a World of HATE. It then depends on which World you choose to see: the Ruler of this World or the Ruler of all of Eternity.

To appreciate the truth, you must understand the lies.

The thinker is one thing, just as a planner is another. He who can do both is the true essence of wisdom. Servant Leaders understand the importance of being able to do both. Those who try to control/rule will be oblivious to these qualities, even if they are right under their nose. A lot of people think leadership is about power and control. Thus, they feel like just because they have a title, it entitles them to display their rule. The mistake in this logic is that without people to lead, there would not be a leader. A leader is only as good as the people they lead. A show of might belittles those who are under the ruler and what eventually happens is people start to rebel against the control.

A true leader knows how to relinquish his control to those whom he serves, as this is where true leadership bonds are formed. Neither power nor control will be sustained over time, as these are merely weak bonds built upon a feeling of superiority. Those who understand the importance of being an enabler of the talents of the people they serve will allow them to be a vital part of the team's success. If you want to truly be a leader, empower and enable the people around you. Inclusion is where the best and brightest lights get their shine. Be willing to dim your light just a little and see how much of a difference it will make in others.

Understand that there are works that come along with leadership. Servants understand that their works come from a place of selflessness. Thus, a servant leader is one who will strive for the bottom as opposed to the popular style of wanting to be on the top. They know that being on the top will come as a result of uplifting those who are on the bottom. This is because servants understand that the only place that you are able to see and include all people is through being willing to see things from all levels. Being at the top removes you from the very people you are trying to lead. It creates a chasm between the leader of the work that needs to be done and the workers who are doing the work.

READ
Matthew 23:11-12
Luke 22:26
Mark 10:43-45

There are two types of works people do in the world today: those that are of the Lord All Mighty and those that are of the enemy. Take the time today to look in the mirror and ask this question, "How is what I am doing impacting how I feel towards others in the world?" If the answer leads you to a good space deep down inside, open up and consider how your works have impacted others around you. If it does not lead to good feelings, change it immediately! The works of the Lord are the types of work that may not pay you a single dime in terms of money; however, when you submit your timesheets at the end of the day, your heart is full of joy, love, peace, passion, patience, happiness, etc.

On the other hand, works of the enemy may have big monetary or financial rewards, but at the end of the day, you may have to do some things that were not as ethical, not as loving, not as honest, or not purely focused on serving The Kingdom of Heaven and its divine purpose. The results of trying to get around the truth is always a lie. No matter what way we may try to spin it, it is still a lie. These types of work tend to leave the pocketbooks happy, but the heart is still empty.

You keep trying to open a door that the Lord has closed on you, and that is why you keep failing. You've tried everything you know to be true, and it is still not working. It is time to look in the mirror and realize His Will, and understand why the door closed in the first place. He's closing that door so you will understand that your will is contrary to His Will. When everything you thought you knew failed, turn to Him, and the right doors will swing wide open. However, it will require you to give up something or deny yourself and step out on Faith.

READ | James 1:23-25

If you have found yourself going back and forth between these two things, as I have before, it is time to submit your letters of confession to the Most High and commit yourself to fulfilling out His Purpose/Will. Abandon the detestable things in this world that are designed to keep you from glory. Don't put it off until later. THE TIME IS NOW! You do not have until later to try to finally get it right because the present may just be the last opportunity you get.

Remember, you do not have to fight every battle, though. Faith will bring you through! Watch out for those who are experts in words. Do not allow them to drag you into their world of hatred with negative thoughts or words. They are just looking for a weak soul with vulnerable faith to bring along with them into a World that they do not belong in. Remember, they will not win. They are experts in planting doubt, just like a seed on weak soil. Do not allow these seeds to grow in your soil of Great Faith. Your faith has been rooted in good, virtuous soil with the Master, and you can feel it in your heart when they are telling you things that do not feel/seem right. God has already taken care of these battles for you, so have faith that this, too, shall pass.

READ
Exodus 14:14
Isaiah 49:25
Psalms 35:1, 109:3
Proverbs 15:18, 20:3
2 Timothy 2:23

I say this to you if it makes you happy momentarily but causes others to stumble, struggle, feel pain, hurt, cry, etc., and turn away from those works now. The present time is the only time guaranteed to you, so turn now from the ways of the enemy and put yourself in a position to receive the love that you so desperately seek to find. Let the promise of peace abode in your life as you start to do the works of righteousness.

Thank you for all of my trials and tribulations. Without them, I wouldn't appreciate your blessings as much as I do.

CHAPTER III

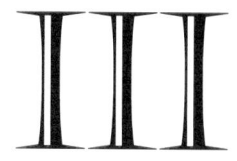

"THE CHANGE YOU ARE CALLING FOR STARTS WITH US"

"My brothers and sisters, believers in our glorious Lord Jesus Christ must not show favoritism."
(James 2:1, NIV)

CHAPTER 3
"The Change You Are Calling For Starts With Us"

A lot of the biggest challenges in life stem from the struggle to break generational curses. A true testament is when you examine the cycles of previous generations and how much of an impact they have on your current behaviors. You start to see them in the mistakes you have made in the past and the current results that you are getting. If you can make these examinations with truth, you can then start the process of discerning your actions going forward. Your future does not have to die with your past, but it requires you to dare to be different. Breaking the cycle starts when you examine your past!

Accept it for what it is, move forward, and never look back.

As I think back through the days of my hypocrisy, I realize that I did not always "Walk It Like I Talk It," as the Migos would say. I found myself repeatedly thanking the Creator for his Mercy and Grace. It was not by my deeds that He kept me because if that were the case, He would have given up on me a long time ago, but it was through His gifts that He kept me. The reality is that I did not always walk the walk, although I did sometimes talk the talk. In my previous years, I have discovered that only a fool talks of things he is not disciplined enough to do himself, for it is through actions that words become meaningful, not through words alone.

In my maturity, I strive toward being an example of the words I believe. This is where strong faith comes in. The moment I fail to exemplify these things is the moment that I make my beliefs out to be a lie. I'm just glad that He saw beyond my past actions and decided to search my heart instead. In understanding these things, my goal becomes showing actions as opposed to saying sweet words. Through actions, the words gain validity. Through my character, the things I know to be true come to fruition. If I say that I believe in The Light, then I should strive to be an example of The Light that lives within me. This is my goal!

These scriptures are working on me.

READ
James 1:26-27
James 2:1-12
James 3:13-18
James 4:1-10

Be aware of your thoughts; they shape your life. Want to change your life? CHANGE your mind frame.

Give your full effort into everything you do. Understand that failure is a part of the process, but there is a greater purpose. Strive for greatness and help pass this greatness along to those whom you encounter. You will find that your priorities will change, and that is not necessarily a bad thing. It is time to make the choice of living for the right purpose.

"Lord, order my steps. Control who comes into my life and who leaves my life. The past is your seed, preparing you for growth. Allow me to grow past the context in which you met me in."

What you are going through will not kill you because you are a child of The Most High God. When you take less and do more with it, you know you are destined for greatness. It's something about survivors that attracts them to other survivors. Your praise is a direct result of your pain.

READ | 2 Samuel 9

One of the basic disciplines of "CHANGE" is recognizing that there is a need for it.

The thing about change and growth is that both can be forced down your throat. For a brief time, you will appear to show some of the characteristics of both, but growth and change are two things that take time to truly embrace. Over time, the truth will come out, and people who really know you will know if this is who you really are or if you are just going through the motions. Words must have actions behind them for them to be trusted. Your core and mindset must be right. If you claim to want these things, you will have to start thinking differently in order for you to change and grow. Mindset is what maintains them. A true desire for these two will dwindle over time if you are forced to change/grow, and it is not in the heart/mind of the person it is forced upon. They must want change and strive for it themselves in order to truly grow. That said, do not try to force people to change or grow. If they want it, you will see and feel it. Their words will match their actions/intentions.

If you are struggling with getting in shape, overcoming smoking, being healthier, getting rid of old habits, getting out of situation-ships, or anything else in life, it starts with your MINDset. That's where your starting point must come from. A paradigm shift is the key to overcoming all these things. How you view things will change how you react to them. Take back control today! Change your MIND and change your life. Just think about it.

Be open to being honest about how you see others as well. Bias is a part of everyone. The key is not reacting to those biases but using your ability of discernment to process and eliminate those feelings. This is something that a racist, sexist, or bigot struggles with being able to do. Some people never achieve the ability of discernment. Ask yourself this simple question, "What type of person are you? Are you the person who wears their biases on their sleeve or the type that uses their brain to process their biases and treat people as human life?

As you continue to open your eyes, you will notice how much more closed off you become, and you will begin to focus on what is important. You will begin to see the vision so clearly that you can never close your eyes to the lies anymore. Changes are imminent, and you must have no problem with making them continue on the path to righteousness. Be strong. Sunny days are up ahead. Seek His strength and understanding, and He will guide you through it all. There is only one thing that God cannot do, and that is fail! Just know that He has a purpose and calling in your life. Although we often fall short of being the perfect creatures that He created us to be, He will see us through all things if we turn to Him and listen to Him through His word!

Looking through different lenses could change your outlook on life. Don't be afraid to get outside of your comfort zone. I changed the view, and now I see clearly.

CHAPTER IV

NOT ALLOWING THE PAST TO CONTROL YOUR FUTURE

"He shall say: 'Hear, Israel: Today you are going into battle against your enemies. Do not be fainthearted or afraid; do not panic or be terrified by them.'"
(Deuteronomy 20:3, NIV)

CHAPTER 4
Not Allowing the Past to Control Your Future

Do not allow your past to control your future. Stop holding on to the past and let the past be the past. It cannot hurt you in the future unless you allow it to control you. Forgive and let go! You cannot be fighting harder for other people's problems than they do. It is unhealthy to walk with people who do not want to get better themselves. You must learn to pick your battles. Remain true to who you are, and continue to have faith. Don't miss out on your blessings trying to please people. HASHEM ELOHIM (God) gives us a lot of power as beings created in His image, but in this power, we also can become too self-aware. This awareness turns quickly into ego, which leads us to boast about what "WE" have done. Just that quick, "WE" think that "WE" have all the power while forgetting where the power was granted from.

READ
Genesis 1:26-27
Deuteronomy 20:3-4

It was along this same logic that Moshe (Moses) and Aharon (Aaron), two of El Shaddai's (Lord Almighty's) chosen ones, missed getting to the promised land. Just before striking the rock with the staff twice, causing water to spring forth to silence the grumbling of the chosen people, their words to the people were, "Must 'WE' fetch you water out of this rock?" This was glorifying in the presence of the people to Moshe and Aharon, but by not Glorifying the One who gave them the power and the commandments to use it, they committed one of the greatest mistakes that can be made. They glorified themselves as though it was their own hands or powers that caused the water to come from the rock.

I have been guilty of these same foolish mistakes before myself. After having the Holy Spirit come over me in the Dominican Republic while sitting down at the table with one of the enemy's workers, I foolishly took credit for the power that was bestowed upon me while I was there with a friend. As Satan, whom I sat down at the table with, tried to explain to me that it would take me a few years before I would come into the righteousness of God due to my messiness, the Spirit began to speak. What came from my mouth was the truth about his ways and actions, which we had experienced with him time after time while being in the Dominican Republic on vacation. By the end of speaking this truth, he was in such a rush to get away from the table and leave the condominium that he left behind a few of his items.

That is when my friend, who had gotten up from the table out of fear for the things that took place in the room, came back over to the table and said, "Maaan, did you just see that?" It was in that moment, out of ignorance about what had just taken place that I began to boast as though it was me who made these things happen.

I will save the rest of this spiritual experience in my following literary works, along with the peculiar photos taken from that night. In hindsight, after being baptized, studying tons of hours, and coming to an understanding of His Words, I now know that this experience had nothing to do with my power whatsoever and had all to do with the Power of His Holy Spirit. As beings, we are quicker to marvel and wonder over the painting while neglecting that it is the work of The Painter.

The moral of the story is this: remember that in all things, no matter how big or small, all the Glory goes to the Creator who gives you the little power you have. So, in all your boasting, do not forget to boast ecstatically to the Giver of Power. This way, you will not block your future blessings/powers. Do not take your gifts for granted. Salvation and mercy are extremely valuable gifts for you to just throw away. If you just so happened to receive them, be careful what you do going forward. If only you knew the depths of the gift you received this morning by being able to open your eyes, you would correct that attitude you choose to walk around with.

READ
Numbers 20:10-12
Deuteronomy 31:1-2

Don't wait until you are on your deathbed to figure out what is important in life. By that time, it will be too late.

My youngest son and I finished the book of Daniel together the other night. This was our first complete book in the bible, and now we are reading about David at my son's request. He was astonished by the Power of the Living God that was with the faithful people. I'm amazed that he was able to recall as much as he was after our readings each night. It took us seven nights, but it was worth the time. It's truly wonderful what he can do when he focuses on things. I am teaching my kids the things I wish I would have known when I was younger and breaking the generational curses in today's society. Teaching them to free their minds will help them learn on their own so that they do not become an "Indentured Servant" of this world!

Even if things didn't work out the way that you thought they should have, it was purposeful for all things to happen for the greater good.

READ | Proverbs 16:3-4

Even though none of us are perfect, we could at least practice it while we still have the chance. None of us are perfect by any means, but at least we can strive to get better and better each day. Each day is a perfect day to try it out. You may have some failures but pausing to pray will help you through the troubles of each day. Step by step, hour by hour, moment by moment, it is an opportunity to see what others do not see. Allow Him to guide your steps. He will NEVER fail! It was You (The Most High Lord) pulling me through!

In all your works, do not forget to give thanks to The Giver of these works. Do not be too proud of the handy works of one's own hands, so much so that you forget Who gave you your hands in the first place. This craftiness of man's hands will surely block you from the blessings He has in store for you.

If you are speaking on me based on past experiences, just know that you don't know me, and likewise.

CHAPTER V

THE KID WHO MADE IT OUT OF THE SLUMS

"But as for me, I watch in hope for the Lord, I wait for God my Savior; my God will hear me."
(Micah 7:7, NIV)

CHAPTER 5
The Kid Who Made It Out of the Slums

Other people have used me for personal gain in much of my life. I can remember the age of ten when I would work with my stepdad. We would make money together mowing yards or raking leaves. After finishing a job, he would ask to borrow some of my hard-earned money with the promise of returning it. It was not until later that I found out that he would buy drugs with it, and this was why I would never see it again. People still use me to this day to feed others off the plate that was furnished to them. I have never asked anyone for anything but their LOVE and honesty because I give wholeheartedly, but one thing I do know is that what happens in the dark will eventually come to light. All I ever ask from anyone is to be honest with me because I can respect and work with honesty.

People often wonder why I am so positive, and my reply is simple, "It's because I've been through sooo much in life." From no running water, living on the Southside of Nashville, AR, with a population of five thousand, including cows and dogs, until now. Even at the age of five, The Lord was guiding me. I lived with my grandparents in my early childhood, where there was an outhouse as a toilet. We would have to tote water from across the street just to have clean drinking water and a means of taking a bath. My grandfather was a farmer, the descendant of a slave, and a former sharecropper.

Yes, he was a farmer, mechanic, electrician, plumber, carpenter, and landscaper. Yes, he picked cotton alongside my grandmother before all these things! Yes, my grandfather had a garden, and in the middle of it was an apple tree. "Thank you" to the ones who came before us for all they taught us and for the ones after us who are teaching us as we speak! As always, Glory to The One above for His Anointed One and for building us the way that He did! I'm a proud ancestor of A Slave.

My childhood was filled with many loving moments. Even though I did not have much by this world's standard, the one thing I was always rich in was LOVE. Although we were poor, I never knew it. We always had a meal on the table, although the roaches and rats ate from the same table. My grandfather had three gardens, and he would grow almost all the food that we ate. I can even remember shelling Purple-Hull Peas as a young boy and my other cousins getting mad at me because of my short attention span, which often led to me starting with them but rarely finishing. My grandmother, Maw-Maw, would fix us sausage and biscuits every morning. She did not miss a single day. After cooking each morning, she and Pawpaw would enjoy their daily cup of Folger's Coffee.

Pawpaw was also a mechanic who could fix or build almost anything. I remember the room he used to sleep in, which he built and added to the back of the old wooden and tin house. Although he did not finish it, he slept in the part that was livable up until he found a snake in our home. This is when he moved to a room toward the front. He also was an expert in carpentry and was one of the best at mowing a yard. He had even cleared an area just to the east of the house that had grown tall with bushes. This was one of the many ways he would make a little extra money on the side. He mowed almost all the people in the neighborhood's lawn. They could almost count on the fact that if Mr. Haze were coming to mow their lawn, he would have his grandson with him. They would always talk to me and give me candy to eat. This was such a part of the routine that Pawpaw had even built a wagon that he could pull behind his lawnmower so that I could ride along.

My grandfather was very stern, though. I think this is where I got a lot of my stubbornness from. When he said something, that is what he meant. I can remember a time from my childhood when he used almost every form of discipline on the grandkids, except for my cousin Tee and me. The others always called us the favorites because we did not get in as much trouble as they did. This is because we were the grandkids who listened and rarely disobeyed what our parents and grandparents told us. For the most part, we behaved, especially when the switches or belts would come out. Not that we were perfect by any means; in fact, I can even remember a time when I was throwing rocks inside the house, and I put a big hole in my mother's fish tank that she loved so much. She was so mad and wanted to spank me, but Pawpaw would not let her whip me.

When I was around the age of four, one of our cousins was down for the summer from Kansas City. It was a scorching summer day, and my grandfather had left the house early in the morning, but before he left, he provided us with specific instructions. The old house had a wooden screen door, which was used to keep all the bugs out of the house as well as to provide a little ventilation since we did not have air conditioning. However, the door would not stay closed by itself and my grandfather had made a wooden plank to temporarily hold the door closed until he could fix it when he arrived back home that evening. His instructions that morning were that no one mess with the plank that he had put in place to hold the door closed so that he could fix it after he returned.

One of my older cousins decided that he would ignore what Pawpaw had said. For some reason, he decided to take the wooden plank and throw it away. I'm not sure if he did it on purpose or if it was an accident and I still haven't found out to this day. Now, our cousin, who was down for the summer, was the only person who saw him do this, unbeknownst to the rest of us. There were six of us grandkids there that summer, including our cousin from Kansas, and we had been playing at the house all day. It was not until later in the evening that our grandfather returned home.

The first thing that he noticed was that the plank, which he had specifically told us not to touch, was missing from the front door. All of the grandkids who regularly stayed with our grandparents knew that our grandfather was not the type of person that you played with, and you never lied to him regardless of what happened. He called all of us inside, as we had all been playing outside, around the house. The first question he asked when he arrived was, "Who touched that plank that I put on the screen door that I told y'all not to move?" No one answered. He then went around to all the grandkids individually and repeated the same question to us.

After not getting an answer from anyone in the room, he called all of us back outside. See, Pawpaw was committed to getting the truth out of us, one way or the other. The reality was that there were only two people who knew what had happened to the plank, one of whom was the guilty party, but neither of them was going to confess. So, Pawpaw grabbed a switch off one of the many trees we had around the yard and then commanded us to all line up from youngest to oldest. He asked the question again, "Now, who touched that plank?" Again, no one answered. At this point, Tee and I were excluded from the lineup since Maw-Maw had confirmed what we told him, which was that we had been in the house all day.

Pawpaw began to whip the entire line. At first, no one cried, and no one told who had moved the plank. Pawpaw then took off his belt. The same question came again, "So, who touched the plank?" Again, he got no response, so he went down the line again. This time, everyone cried except for our two oldest cousins, but Pawpaw still did not get the truth from us. He then grabbed an extension cord. He started again, from youngest to oldest. This time, everyone was crying except for our oldest cousin. You could tell that he was more angry than anything else. "So, no one knows what happened to the plank?" Pawpaw said. This time, my oldest cousin spoke up out of anger. "We didn't touch your stick!"

This is when things changed. "Speak up, son; you got something to say?" Pawpaw then commanded me to get his bullwhip off his workbench. So, I walked over slowly, hoping that someone knew who had moved the plank and that they would step up and tell Pawpaw what happened. When I arrived back with the whip, I handed it over to my grandfather. "Pawpaw, you better not hit me with that whip!!," said my oldest cousin out of a fit of anger. "PaawPaaw!!!!" WHAAAAM!! All you could hear was screaming as my cousin cried out in agony as the whip touched his backside. He was no longer the toughest one in the bunch.

After all the pain and anguish that took place, my grandfather never did get the truth out of us that day. It was not until after our cousin from Kansas had returned home that we learned who had actually touched the plank. Although it was horrible at the time, as I look back at that day, there was a bigger lesson that was taught. My grandfather was committed to seeking the truth from us, so much so that he was willing to submit us to extreme pain. Even though I was not a part of the actual pain, I felt the pain of my cousins.

These lessons would follow me for years. Lies bring you pain that only the truth can save you from. It was not until my thirties that I realized the importance of these lessons. It took me a lot of stumbling to realize that it is much better to be honest with people, no matter how they will take it. Not only are you doing them a favor, but you are also saving yourself a lot of time and heartache by being honest with them.

A liar will steal, and a thief will murder. Actions and words can be murderous, so be sure to keep them in truth and light.

Another one of the most memorable moments I have from my early childhood is of a time when I was the one disobeying my grandfather. I have explained to you the agony that I witnessed surrounding the circumstances with the wooden plank. I also mentioned that my grandfather would take me almost everywhere he went. It was a regular occasion to see me with him while he did yard work for the people in the neighborhood. On one particularly sweltering summer day, Pawpaw was going just around the corner to mow a lady's yard who I had previously visited with him before. This day, however, he told me not to come with him and to stay at home. He had given me specific instructions only to ride my bike in front of the house and not to go any further. As I always did, I agreed to his orders.

I decided to ride my bike from one corner to the next. As I rode to the far end of the street, the sound of Pawpaw's lawn mower began to become faint, but as I came back by the house, I could hear the sound louder and louder. Ever since seeing the pain of my cousins the summer before, I would not even say a single word against anything my grandfather would say, let alone disobey a direct order.

As I rode my bike that day, I began to get bored. Normally, I would just play with my other toys in the front yard, but something told me differently that day. Something kept telling me to just ride by our neighbor's house, even though I knew what the consequences would be if my grandfather were to see me. For some reason, I never gave it a second thought. I turned my bike around and rode by the alley. As I approached the alley to look for my grandfather, this is when I saw him slumped over the steering wheel with the lawnmower still running. He was having a heat stroke.

As soon as I saw him, I peddled my bike as fast as I could down the alley toward him. When I arrived there, I called his name and there was no response. I then tried to shake him to see if he was sleeping. Now, I was only five years old at this point, and I had never experienced anything like this before, so I did not really know what to do. I turned off the lawnmower and went to the backdoor of the lady's house and began to pound on the door hard. At this point, it was no later than one o'clock in the afternoon, and I was not getting an answer. I knocked a second time, and finally, after about five minutes, the neighbor answered the door. "Hey baby, what is it?" she asked. "It's Paw-Paw; I can't wake him up!" I replied. She looked around the corner to see him still in the condition that I had found him in. She immediately dialed 9-1-1 and rushed down the steps to help him out. The 9-1-1 operator had told her to give him something warm to drink, so she went back to her house to start some coffee. She told me to rush back home and let Maw-Maw know that she had already called 9-1-1.

By the time I arrived back home to get my grandmother and returned to the neighbor's house, the ambulance was just arriving. They loaded my grandfather into the back and rushed him to the hospital. I was unaware at the time, but this was not my grandfather's first time dealing with heat exhaustion. Later that day, when my mom arrived, we all loaded into the car and went to the emergency room. Since I was a child, I had to wait for a while in the lobby before I could go back to see Pawpaw. It seemed like forever! Finally, the doctor came out and told us that he was in stable condition. He then asked, "Who was the one that found him?" That is when everyone pointed toward me. He then begins to tell the family that if Pawpaw had been out there for another ten to twenty minutes, he probably would have died. He went on to call me a hero.

When I arrived in the room to see Pawpaw, he gave me a big hug and told me that I was his angel. He never mentioned anything about the fact that I disobeyed him or anything about my punishment for doing so. He just thanked me and told me that an angel was watching over him that day. To this day, who knows why I decided to go against my grandfather's words and ride my bike down that road, but I am thankful that I did.

In my adult life, I have come to realize that God works in mysterious ways, and we may never know when He calls us to do His works. I never considered myself a hero or even thought of it in that manner. I was just a five-year-old who happened to be in the right place at the right time, but as I grew to understand more about the spirit, it assigned a new meaning to the reason why I disobeyed a direct order that I knew would potentially bring me so much pain. The spirit leads to all kinds of good places for all who are willing to follow.

Fast forward to when I was sixteen, which was the year that I experienced my first heartbreak in a relationship. This was the first real relationship that I was in and as many of you have experienced as well, I was in the "puppy love" phase. My girlfriend and I worked together at our very first official job and although she lived in the town over, we saw each other frequently. I would even drive to see her on my days off. I was falling in love, even though my views of what love was at that point were very premature.

After a few months, I noticed that she was becoming increasingly distant. I had even heard a few rumors from people in her town that she was seeing a guy that I had known as a good friend. Of course, I was naïve, though, since I had never experienced anything like this before. I did not know what confrontation was or how to address something like this. It was not until a few weeks later that I saw it with my very eyes. I was completely crushed! I could not believe what I was seeing. There she was, the girl who I thought I was in love with, kissing and holding hands with another guy! My heart sank as I looked on in disbelief. I was hurt. I did not know how to react, so I just turned away and waited until she called to bring it up. Of course, she tried to lie about it at first, but once I told her that I saw them, she confessed.

It was from that point that I began to hurt every woman I encountered. I was the worst of the worst. I would lie, cheat, and deceive women as if it was a game. I said to myself, I will never give a woman the fullness of my heart again. This went on throughout most of my twenties. Woman after woman, lie after lie. It was not until I had some tragic events happen in my life that I realized that life was too short to continue to live the way I was living. Since I was hurt, I went through my life hurting other people. It was not until I lost my brother (who was more like a son to me) that I realized how hurt I was. From the moment of having my heart broken, I never looked in the mirror. Thus, I would push the very hurt I was experiencing onto the people I claimed to care about. All alone, I did not realize that the person I was really hurting was myself. In my selfishness, I hurt many good people, including myself.

Thought: The moment your heart begins to break is also the moment it begins to heal. The mere signs of heartbreak are when you start the process of learning how to heal. With healing comes strength, which is greater than the original state of the heart. It is through a broken heart that you can see the true character. It's up to you to realize all the brokenness lying within and choose how you mend it going forward. How will you use the situations you have been in or are going through?

After those moments of struggle and many more in between, I finally found myself. It took many years of searching and roaming throughout this world to release the hurt that I was holding on to in my heart. September 20, 2017, marked the day of my rebirth through The Savior by getting baptized in water. I can say it has been quite an experience ever since that moment. It has altered my life experience tremendously in ways I never would have imagined.

First of all, 2018 was a crazy year! There were so many changes in my life, so many ups and downs. As I look back, I know that every last bit of it was purposeful. With sooo much death that year and the fact that I went to sooo many funerals, my entire outlook on life changed. Seemed like every time I received a news notification or got on social media, I saw sooo many R.I.P. posts. It became hard to even get online and make a post or look at a notification on my phone. From family members to close friends, to classmates, and even a fellow employee, it seemed to be more and more common.

Personally, I have experienced so many levels of loss in one year that it would make the average person question every essence of what this thing called life is supposed to be about. I've lost material things, cars, loved ones, money, positions, family, and I've even lost friends. Through all I have lost, there is one thing I gained, FAITH! The losses cannot even begin to come close to all that I have gained in that year of rebirth. After all, they say you have to lose yourself in order for you to find God.

In finding Him, I experienced more great and exciting things in one year than I did in all of the previous years of my life, and this was just the beginning. He blessed me in such a way that I have been able to be a blessing to many others, and He has shown me that none of it would have been possible without His Will. Hallelujah to The Almighty Creator for His grace, mercy, and salvation!

Through it all, He has proven what He will do for His faithful! So, in writing this message, my encouragement to you is to find faith in all things, know that He is with you, and when He does exactly what He said He would do, do not forget to Glorify Him! Glory to the Creator for sending a Savior into this world to be a guide for those who believe! May He continue to strengthen the faith of the weak! My hope is that this message inspires you to keep the faith and glorify the Lord Almighty!

MINI STORIES

"There is only one Lawgiver and Judge, the one who is able to save and destroy. But you—who are you to judge your neighbor?"
(James 4:12, NIV)

MINI STORIES

The Day I ate a Big Ole Slice of Humble Pie

The same things that I told my kids they needed to do, I failed to do myself. After talking to them one night about not ever calling me, a conversation we have had in the past many times, the very next day, my mom sent me a text saying, "Do you know you have a mother? You can call or text every now and then to say hey, or I am still alive, or something bigger! Love you." It was at that moment that I realized that I had been the biggest "HYPOCRITE" to my children. Let's just say I had to swallow my own words and apologize to them for how I had not been the right role model. I was not modeling the very behavior that I expected from them, and God had a very ironic way of letting me see my moments of hypocrisy. I even let them read the text thread so they would see my mistakes.

The ways of God are absolutely astonishing! I'm extremely thankful that He would correct me in the moment by showing me my own ways. More importantly, I am thankful that He allowed me to use my own faults to teach my kids. I know that I now must show them an example of the changes moving forward to rebuild their trust. Thank you, Lord, for your moments of revelation. Thank you, Mother, for the "Love you!" text to remind me that God's continuing His works.

Live each day to its fullest. The only thing that passes by is time, so find your purpose and live for it every day before time passes you by.

Strength in Faith

A while back, I was told that the place I had put in so much of my time, blood, sweat, and tears was getting ready to close its doors. This meant that I would have to find another position within the company if I wanted to continue to work there. It was a moment of utter disbelief because I always knew in the back of my mind that this day could come, but until it happened, I always felt like my job was secure and that we had nothing to worry about. For all of you who have lost your job or been laid off, you know the feeling I am talking about.

The good news, though, was that most of the employees were going to still have their jobs as the transition was happening. They were offered the option to be able to work from home or move to another location if they met the requirements. This meant that they would have a few months to relocate if they did not want to work from home. My position, on the other hand, was being eliminated on the closing date of the center, which was a few months away. If I wanted to stay with the company, I would have to interview and be accepted for another position before the deadline. Otherwise, I would have to accept a separation package, which was a fairly good amount of money, by the way, if I didn't find a position by the closure date.

I had just gotten to a point in my career where I really felt like I was having a profound impact on the business. I was excelling at my position, so much so to the point where I was being specially requested at various locations within the company. I developed several special projects and achieved the highest level of ratings in our yearly reviews. To top it off, I really loved what I was doing. I felt like I was having a real impact, not only on the business but on the lives of the people who I was so graciously able to touch.

Reluctantly, I decided to look for other positions within the company. That's when I came across the position that I had interviewed for several times in the past but was eventually turned down. This was a position that I really wanted because it was within the same department that I was currently in, but it had a larger responsibility. In this new role, I would now be responsible for training people who were hired to do my old job that I loved so much. I prayed and prayed about the decision to put in the application. After waiting for the response, I moved forward with applying for the position. A few days later, I received an email with a request for an interview.

I had prepared myself both mentally and spiritually for the interview process. Even my family and friends had prayed for me as well, but I was still nervous about interviewing for the position again. After all, this was a position I really wanted and one that I had interviewed for in the past without any success. You know how it is: we all would like to believe that we have faith, but until a situation comes that really puts us to the test, we really do not know how strong our faith is. Plus, there was a lot riding on me getting this job. My family was depending on me, and I was under a lot of pressure to come through for them as I had in the past. The funny thing about the mind is that it can be your best or worst enemy. We want to believe that we are good enough, but failure wants us to believe that it may happen again. Although I had all of this experience and all of this practice, that thought of the last time I had interviewed for this position was at the back of my mind.

READ
Matthew 17:20, 21:21-22
Hebrews 11

So, the day of the interview arrives, and I get on the phone with a person named Shawn. My thought process before the call was, who is this guy I am going to have to impress? I log in to the conference call five minutes before the start time and am the first person on the line. A female voice comes on and says, "I'm Shawn," then proceeds to tell me about the confusion around her name. That is when I explained to her that I understood because I get the same thing when people see my name as Nikia. It was at that moment that I realized that I was guilty of judging before I met the person. The very thing that I have told others not to do, I had done myself. I was guilty of judging a book by its cover, so to speak. The moral of the story is, "Don't be so quick to judge others." You never know who that person is until you get to know them.

READ | James 4:12

Let's just say that God allowed me to have the best interview that I have ever had throughout my entire career. It was on a Friday when I had my interview, and as it ended, I was told that they still had a few other candidates to go through and that I would hear something by the following week. I had a few other interviews scheduled for that week for positions that I really did not want, but I wanted to keep my options open just in case I did not get the position. Shortly after the interview, I received an email with an invite titled "Interview Feedback." It was scheduled for the following Monday morning at nine.

Now, you know me, I was overthinking and stressing out because, in my mind, "Interview Feedback" meant that I did not get the job. So, Monday rolls around, and I get on the call and there are two other managers on the bridge with me. We are still waiting for the third person to join. The vibe in the room was all happy on their end, but I was still nervous to see what the feedback was. That's when the third person joins the call and apologizes for being late. She then starts by telling me that she would like to extend me a job offer! Now, you can imagine how shocked I was at that moment. I almost cut her off from finishing the rest of the conversation to thank her for the opportunity.

Something that I learned over the years, before you make up your mind about something, take one last moment and ask yourself, "What about God?" Without the answer to this question, you will surely fail if your will is not in alignment with God's Will. I've been on the wrong side of this question many times. Most of the time, I did not immediately fail overnight. He allowed me to go down my own stubborn path for years, in some cases, before I failed. This is one of His Guarantees, the promise of free will. This is a choice that is given to all human beings, and we are all free to choose between right and wrong. In making my choices, I had to realize that a lot of the ones I had made in my past were not the right ones. I had to come to the realization that a lot of my failures were due to going against His Holy Will. I had to learn the hard way. If only I had taken the time in the past to understand what His Will was. Make sure you take the time to consider this question in all the decisions you make, "What About God?"

I am thankful that He hears our requests, even when our brain wants us to think that He doesn't. Faith is belief in things that are unseen. It is by faith that we are granted the gifts of mercy and salvation. When we cannot see how things are going to work out, if you take it to Him, just have faith in knowing that it is taken care of. This does not mean it is going to work out exactly the way you thought it should. It means that His Will is being done! This was a moment that really strengthened my faith. It showed me the importance of humility by allowing Him to take command of things and brought me a newfound perspective on the importance of prayer.

READ
Judges 18:1-6
Micah 7:7
Romans 5:3-11
Colossians 1:9-14

Glory to the Creator for keeping me in my moments of foolishness. Although I did not deserve it, God saw the best in me!

After these tragedies in my life, I committed to no longer being the person I had been most of my twenties. After taking a long look in the mirror, I realized that the person I had become was not the person that I wanted to be. Now, there were many things that I put myself through in leading up to this realization, including cheating and getting caught up several times, custody battles with the mothers of my children, marriage and divorce, judging others for their ways, etc., just to name a few. All of those stories I will save for a different book, but I want you to know that a lot of the pain I experienced was a direct reflection of the actions that I took.

People will never realize the damage they are doing to others until similar situations start happening to them. You cannot do wrong or continue to just take advantage of people/things and expect good in return. Focus on doing right in every facet of life. Be happy with doing your best. You cannot do dirt and expect it not to come back on you. It may not be today, it may not be tomorrow, it may not be next year, but it will eventually come back. For this very reason, I try my best to do right by people. I have failed at this goal from time to time, and for anyone I failed, I have apologized and committed to not doing it again. I was wrong!

Regardless of how much hate and disappointment I have experienced in life, I still find a way to find LOVE through everything. It's gotten me into a lot of situations before, both good and bad, but what can I do? It is who I am. "I am not them; they are not me." I LOVE hard.

READ | Galatians 6:7-10

In life, there will be Wins and there will be Learning. For me, there is no Losing, only Learning. The moment you stop Learning, day by day, is the moment the world begins to pass you by. Enjoy every Learning moment because you never know if you will ever get that opportunity again.

God has a funny way of exposing our truths, so why lie? Once you commit to the truth, you must never go back! If there is anyone that I have ever offended or done wrong in the past, I would like to extend my deepest apology from the depths of my Heart. I am truly, deeply sorry and may this apology bring blessings to you in the future!

People often ask, "Why are you so happy? Why are you always smiling?" My reply is simple, "because sometimes a smile is enough to get people through whatever it is that they are going through at the moment." See, for me, people are an investment. You never know when it could be you who needs the smile. Invest in others' emotional bank accounts because you never know when you will be the one needing to make a withdrawal.

What is happiness? I would say that happiness is that split-second decision we have between whether an event, circumstance, or person will control our reactions/behaviors versus being in control of how we view them. For the most part, we are out of control with external things, but we all have a choice on how we view and react to them. We tend to say things such as, "That's a bad situation," or "They are just not a good person," when the reality is that our perspectives could be wrong.

Remember, all things were good before the first deception of mankind, as described in the book of Genesis. There was no such thing as bad, wrong, or evil. As a matter of fact, on the sixth day, The Creator looked upon all that He had created and exclaimed that it was "Very Good." So, if you cannot control the situation, which a lot of times is out of your hands, why not choose how you perceive the situation. By doing this, you will see that your reactions to the things that used to have control over you will be different. You will start to have more control over your happiness, and things that used to get you down will slowly decrease. Remember, your reaction to things is controlled by one of two forces: good or evil. Don't allow the works of the enemy to control how you react to situations or to control who you become. All of this is a choice, so choose a better way.

READ | Genesis 1:31, 3:1-19

Don't allow hatred to prevail in a loving heart. Those two feelings were never meant to reside in the same space.

Take the time to pause before you react to things. If your view of a situation is bad, I challenge you to see it differently. You will be surprised at how God will change the world around you once you choose to see events, circumstances, and people differently. What choices will you make today?

I have been through more than anyone can imagine. If I can make it through, I know you can also. God has blessed me beyond my wildest dreams, and if I had listened to Him before, there is no telling where I would be. I had to learn things the hard way, which has led me to become the person I am today. For this simple reason, I must go hard at everything I do. He gave me a new lease on life through His gift of Salvation, so to not use my new freedom to do righteousness and Glorify Him would be a disgrace! My kids deserve to be better than me, and I will spend every ounce of time, money, effort, and heart making sure that they will be.

As the years have passed and we have gotten older, I've come to realize that some of us continue to grow, and others start to show their true character. Some of the words that are used daily bring us together, while others are a continuation of a journey toward division. The more we grow, the more we realize that things and people are the way they are for a reason. God's promise is to those who will listen and take heed! Those who do not listen become masters at keeping the people who do want to listen away from that promise.

READ | James 1:19-27, 4:1-10

Their words entangle us. Their thoughts are planted amongst those who lack the ability to recognize truth. Their television shows promote agendas designed to keep you in the dark. Their cartoons even paint these pictures to our youth. Their messages invoke the very ideals of hatred and division that they want you to believe is how it should be.

All the things I mentioned above were created with a clear purpose in mind. To all who are willing to open their eyes and see the truth about these things, it becomes increasingly clear what the agenda is for those who are of this world. Just like a programmer entering his programming into a computer, it is designed to make you act, feel, and behave in a certain way and, moreover, keep you in the dark about who you are. Meanwhile, with a successful algorithm in place, the people of God are kept in the dark and away from the covenant made to them.

The mind feeds the heart. What we hear, see, touch, and smell has a huge part to do with the thoughts that are received by the brain. The brain then turns these thoughts into feelings. It is for this reason that you must recognize what information is being fed to your mind. You must have the ability to feed yourself and break free from allowing the things of this world to feed you. Take back your control over the promise of free will today by freeing your mind of the negativity and hatred that they push. Why do you think slaves were not allowed to read? Now, go back and read that paragraph again and understand what I am saying to you. Yes, your mind may be challenged by this logic I just brought to you, but I challenge you to find fault in it.

So, allow me to bring you a little bit of the early promises that were made to you and me. This is one of the promises that the world wants to keep you from. The descendants of Yisroel (Israel, The Chosen People) shall become a multitude of nations and be numerous upon the earth. They are the treasures among the people of Earth. The people who were promised the land of milk and honey. They will do anything to keep you away from what is promised to you. Don't fall victim to the rhetoric/noise being used to distract your listening. Remember, the prophecy is already written, and it is not about the color of your skin, sex, background, nationality, religion, Twitter handle, or anything else created for division by man's perspective, for that matter. It's about your heart! No weapons formed will prosper. Please do not take my word for it. Go read it for yourself. Remember, God is LOVE.

Read | Genesis 17:1-8,48 | Jeremiah 31:1-14

In my latter years, I have come to realize that I do not take nearly as much stuff from people as I used to. I am quick to remove myself from any situation that is counterproductive to my peace. There are two types of people: those who thrive off growth and those who are set in their ways no matter what. Trying to find someone with balance is like trying to find the middle class in today's society; they are pretty much nonexistent. You are either rich or poor. Once a person shows you who they are, you must behave accordingly because grown people are going to be grown regardless of what you say, do, or show them. You have to decide whether you can accept people as they are because you will not be able to change them into who you want them to be. You must learn to let people be who they are. Accept them or move forward.

In today's world, closed minds do not open, and open minds do not close. The only thing that is guaranteed is that time keeps passing us by. It is for that reason that it starts to change your view of time and who/what you choose to spend it on. Some things/people become a priority, while others tend to fall by the wayside. You start to appreciate things more and learn to prioritize your life around fruitful goals. Keep in mind that it is of God that those in authority were sent, that you would be able to clearly see the evil ways of many people! Keep your faith, and know the very God whom you serve deserves all His Glory! This is the beginning of a new thing He is about to do amongst the people. We are on the brink of a new beginning, one that will bring peace and prosperity to the faithful. All these things are happening in such a manner that will bring about the Glorification of the One, allowing it to be possible!

    Do not be troubled; only be afraid of doing that which is evil in the sight of The Almighty. Give Him His praises in your times of trouble, as your troubles will not last much longer! Be a sign to the foolish ones of the strength God has bestowed upon you! Love one another as God has loved you!

    As I sit back and reflect on how AWESOME God has been, I realize that I could have been a lot better to Him. He was not my number one goal or priority and the more I reflect on His greatness, I find more failures that I could have avoided by seeking Him above and throughout all things. Every last bit of it had a purpose, though. Without it, I would not appreciate Him as much as I do today. While I prioritize my future goals, I know who will be at the top of my list from this point forward and I also know the ones that will no longer reside in my top priorities. GOD is and will forever be my número uno, and the rest will fall in order according to growth and obtainability.

The more blessings come, the more praying you must do. The storms will come, so continue to weatherproof your vessel. Prayer still works.

CHAPTER VI

A TESTIMONY OF GOD'S PRESENCE AND REVELATION

"The next day, John saw Jesus coming toward him and said, 'Look, the Lamb of God, who takes away the sin of the world!'"
(John 1:29, NIV)

CHAPTER 6
A Testimony of God's Presence and Revelation

God has a peculiar way of showing up when you least expect it. He sends us signs in the strangest ways at times, and He will even show up in different forms. For the longest time, the kids and I were fortunate not to have a neighbor below us in the apartment that we were living in. This meant that we did not really have to worry about disturbing anyone with our playing and noises. This would soon change.

Late one spring, I had some new neighbors move in below me. I had only seen them a few times in passing, but I quickly noticed that one of the first things that they started to do was park in the parking spot that I was used to having. No worries, it was just a parking spot. I took it as a sign that I needed to get a few more steps in, especially since I haven't been running as much as I used to in the past.

I saw the new neighbors several times throughout their move-in process, and each time, it seemed like I had to speak first. Again, this was not a problem for me because you never know what people are going through or what happened that caused them to cross your path. I even saw the man moving items into his place by himself, and I offered to help. He declined my offer with, "Thank you, but I've got it."

It just so happened on the first Saturday after they moved in, it was my weekend to have my kids. My boys are rough, and they love to wrestle and play with each other, as kids typically do. This was a normal part of our weekends together, as it had been in the past. Shortly after they began playing, we received a knock at the door. When I answered the door, there stood the lady from downstairs, and she proceeded to introduce herself to me. In the process of welcoming her to the neighborhood, my youngest and oldest sons came to the door with their arms locked around each other, wrestling. At that moment, I turned to them and told them to stop before they got upset with each other, naïve to the fact that they were stomping on the floor. The lady then left to go back downstairs, and I closed the door.

All of this transpired around midday, and the kids resumed playing as they had always done. A few minutes later, I heard a few loud bangs on the floor below us. It was loud enough to make the boys pause for a second and ask me if I heard it. It then stopped, and the boys continued playing. Suddenly, it started again, and this time, it was louder and for a longer period.

It was at that moment that I realized that banging was the neighbors' way of showing their response to the kids playing on the floor. They had been making a lot of commotion, and this was the neighbor letting us know how loud they were. For those of you who have active kids or have observed kids, you know that it is hard to keep young boys from making a lot of noise at night, and it is even more difficult during the day. Plus, this was something that we had never had a problem within the past, even when we did have people below us. Nevertheless, I got on to the boys and told them to keep it down because we must be mindful of our new neighbors.

As I sat at the table thinking, a few thoughts came to my mind surrounding these events. First, there were approved quiet hours at the complex, which were between the hours of 11:00 PM and 8:00 AM on weekends. Secondly, the lady came up with what I thought was a friendly introduction, but looking back on it, I wondered why she didn't mention anything about the noise at that moment. This pattern of banging on the floor continued several times throughout the months leading up to the events that took place one sweltering summer evening.

Late one Friday night, around 11:30 PM, I was in bed, and I heard loud laughing and talking coming from the room directly below me, which was from the new neighbors that had moved in. My thoughts at the time were that it was after the quiet hours, but I did not complain. Even though the banging, along with how they had chosen to handle the noise, came to mind, I said nothing about these things. I have had neighbors before who were a lot louder than they were, and this had not been a regular thing for them, although it did make me want to rush to judgment quickly.

That Saturday, the kids and I were at home, and they were playing as they always had when the banging started again. At this point, I was fed up with it, so I began to bang on the floor just as they did on the ceiling. Looking back in hindsight, I realized that this was not the right way to manage the situation. Suddenly, the banging stops, and a few moments go by. I then heard a loud knock at my door as though it was the police. My six-year-old asks, "Who is it?" An angry male voice replies, "It's your neighbor; open up!" Not only were my two kids there, but my wife was there also.

I open the door and there stands my neighbor, clearly upset. With an elevated tone, he proceeds to demand that we are extremely loud and that we need to keep it down. After I had informed him about the quiet hours for the complex and the fact that there was a better way to manage the issue, he continued to tell me that it didn't matter that they were kids and that they should be playing outside. The lady then came upstairs, as she could tell that things were getting heated, and this was when I proceeded to inform her of the fact that I had heard them the night before. Instead of managing the noise in the same manner that they had been in the past, as I could have, I decided to ignore it as it seemed like they were having an enjoyable time.

At this point, the man walked downstairs while the lady stayed to share their viewpoint on the issue. I told her that I had been living there for over four years and had never had a complaint. I even considered contacting the office to move to a bottom apartment because I understood their point of view. I also made it a point to let her know that it still was not the right way to manage the issue, especially with my kids observing this entire exchange.

After she left, I had a conversation with my kids about how they should be playing going forward while inside our home. I then told them that they should go outside and play with their neighborhood friends. While they were outside, I talked with my wife about the whole situation and asked her how she felt about how it was handled. We were on the same page, but I did not feel good about my response to the issue. I just did not feel good about it at all. Sitting at my table, I decided to take the situation to God. I prayed for His guidance and for His forgiveness. The kids came back inside shortly after this moment of prayer.

About thirty minutes later, I heard another knock at the door. It was the neighbor again, and this time, he was a lot calmer. He began with this, "I wanted to apologize. God told me to come up here and apologize before the sun sets, and I shouldn't have acted that way." It was at that moment that I realized the true Power of prayer and the timing of God. The Spirit of the Lord had manifested itself as described by Paul in his letter to the Ephesians:

"Therefore, laying aside falsehood, speak truth each one of you with his neighbor, for we are members of one another. Be angry, and yet do not sin; do not let the sun go down on your anger."
Ephesians 4:25-26
(Tyndale House Foundation, 1996, 2004, 2007, 2015)

I reached out my hand, and I pulled him in to give him a hug. I told him, "God is awesome, my brother, and I could have handled it better as well." After all of this, there was one thing that he remembered. He asked me with a smile on his face, "Did you really hear us last night?" I replied, "Yes, it sounded like you all were having fun." He said, "Yes, I was splashing her with water, and I didn't realize you could hear that." He then told me his name and we began to talk about our families and our careers. Believe it or not, we had a lot in common. He had just relocated his family to Arkansas to work for the same company I had worked for prior to starting my current career, and we even knew some of the same people who worked there.

You never know how or when God will show up, but He will always show up if you believe. The Power of prayer is absolutely monumental! God has a mysterious way of showing Himself through others. It could be in the form of a sick person as described in **Luke 13:10-17**, or in the form of a young boy as in **Job 32:6-22**. Even as a man beaten on the side of the road in **Luke 10:30**. Who would have known that my prayers would be answered through someone else speaking what he said God put on his heart?

In conclusion, never allow anger to resonate in your heart. When it sits in your heart for too long, you start to judge the person or the situation. Don't be afraid to ask why. Take the time to get a level of understanding with people. This will help you to think critically about what happened and what could be a better outcome for all. Once the why is provided and understood, you will find that a lot of things that you used to get upset over are no longer bothersome due to you having the understanding, and that is the beginning of love. The meaning of love was best explained in **Luke 10:27**:

"YOU SHALL LOVE THE LORD YOUR GOD WITH ALL YOUR HEART, AND WITH ALL YOUR SOUL, AND WITH ALL YOUR STRENGTH, AND WITH ALL YOUR MIND; AND YOUR NEIGHBOR AS YOURSELF." (Tyndale House Foundation, 1996, 2004, 2007, 2015)

Through the mist of all the filth in this world, there is still beauty. The choice to see it is in the eyes of the onlooker. What is your perspective?

    A few months prior to these events taking place at my home, God revealed Himself in another place. My family and I went to a restaurant after my oldest son's karate event, and we were enjoying a great, rare family moment. No one was on their cell phones, the kids were behaving, and everyone finally came together as a family. I had been through many struggles in the past with being able to get all my kids and their mothers in the same place, other than court, and this was the first time this had happened. I sat back at a table by myself and observed the family as we enjoyed this rare moment in today's world. That is when this elderly couple, whom I had stayed outside to hold the door for earlier, came up to me. The older gentleman approached my table and asked me, "Are you a minister?" I politely replied, "No sir, I train customer service skills as a profession, but what makes you ask if I'm a minister?" He gazed over at my family for a moment and said, "You have a good group of kids, and I have four grandkids, but I can't seem to get them to put their electronics down." I replied, "Well, thank you. They are not perfect, and neither am I. I'm just trying to do the best I can to make sure they are better than me."

It was at that moment that he looked at me and said, "I was a minister for over fifty years." At this point, his wife walked up and introduced herself. She then told me that they had been married for sixty-three years. "Wow, that's a long time. God has truly blessed you all," I replied. Her husband then said, "God is coming! You are a very blessed young man yourself." He went on to tell me about his daughter, who lived in the same city we lived in, and then he asked me about the church that I attended. I told him that I did not currently go to church, but I did take time to read the Word of God. He looked up at me and said, "That's a good thing; God is coming!" I said to him, "Yes, and it's rare moments like these that show that God has not given up on humanity and genuine love!"

I took the opportunity, shook their hands, and told them, "God bless you." Looking back on the entire experience, I go back to the moment when I prayed at the table by myself before I ate my food, giving thanks to God for everything. God places people into your life or on your path for a reason. We may not know what that reason is or the purpose behind it, but everything happens for a reason. Life is about what we learn from it and how we can teach others to be better. The example you set today may just have a lasting impact on someone for a lifetime. What would you want that example to be?

Don't be troubled by trouble. Don't allow circumstances to change your character. Remain true to who you are, and continue to have faith.

It is in some of the happiest moments that you experience some of the darkest storms. In May of 2018, while I was on the trip of a lifetime in Israel, thieves entered my home and took from my earthly possessions. They ravaged my home and left it in shambles, taking what they wanted while leaving behind a path of destruction. It was only through God's Grace and hard work that I was allowed to acquire those material things. So, when they took those blessings, not only were they taking from me, but they were also taking from The One who provided all those things.

That is how the enemy works, though. His goal is to try to distract you from your spiritual connection with The Creator in hopes that you will question God as if He's not greater than every circumstance that takes place here on this earth. He has always provided a way, so who would I be to not praise Him, even in this moment of despair and extreme loss? As I sat outside my home while officers cleared the place, my heart went out to the Lord in prayer. My prayers were not for my possessions or even for myself but for those individuals who committed this act. That's right; my prayers were for the very ones who risked their life to take from the possessions that were provided by The Provider of it all. I prayed that the Lord, who has shown me Mercy throughout my life's struggles; who has granted me Grace through His Love and Compassion, would search their hearts and fulfill His will with the same Mercy and Grace He has shown me.

I was not going to allow anger to overshadow all that I had experienced in The Holy Land by being upset over materialistic things. To do so would be to allow the enemy to have control of me, and that would have allowed him to win his game. My Faith and The Holy Spirit within me would not allow me to go to sleep with that type of anger in my heart. I knew this was just a test. I remembered Job and all that he endured, and I also started to think back to the journey God had just allowed me to experience in The Promised Land. I thought back to the day that the break-in had taken place, and I remembered the experiences I had on my trip. What was very bizarre was the fact that in Tel Aviv, the night that my home was being broken into, a hailstorm passed through that morning around 5:00 AM and woke us all up out of our sleep.

As I reflected on this, a feeling of peace and calm came over my spirit as I remembered the amount of awe and amazement I had experienced while journeying through the country of Israel. I also remembered the fact that I came into this world with nothing, and that is how I will leave it. My Faith in Him who sent me as my Protector and Provider should NEVER be tested by earthly measurements. It was through Job's Faith that he endured, and even though the enemy entered his home and took everything he owned, from his family to his physical health, God restored twice as much as he had before, according to **Job 42**.

Now, I am not Job by any means, but what I know is that He has and will always provide a way for those who come full of Faith, knowing that He works out a plan for the better. Here I am years later as a living testament to His Power, Mercy, Grace, and Salvation. He has done it again! I wrote this testimony in hopes that you may look beyond the circumstances that you are going through today. It is through the toughest heartbreaks that the biggest blessings come to you. Have Faith that He will never put you through more than you can handle, and know that He's developing you for the greatness of His purpose.

On your journey, there will be losses. Understand that it's part of the preparation for your destination. Very few are on the path to where you are headed.

CHAPTER VII

THE WORLD WE LIVE IN TODAY

"Jesus answered, 'I am the way and the truth and the life. No one comes to the Father except through me.'"
(John 14:6, NIV)

CHAPTER 7
The World We Live in Today

In a society where disciplining your child is frowned upon by outsiders, fighting is viral, and instant gratification/attention is what people have come to expect, we still have the audacity to argue about gun control. Yes, this is a profoundly serious topic that needs to be addressed, but the conflict is over how we should address it. As a parent, I'm the first to admit that I've been guilty of exposing some of these things to my own kids, but one thing I can tell you is that my kids know the consequences of even looking at my guns the wrong way, let alone picking them up and doing the unthinkable. What I do know is that too many people have lost their lives or been victims of senseless gun violence, and we still have not even begun to examine many of the issues that are at the root of this problem.

There are a ton of factors involved when it comes to this debate, but almost all of them point toward one direction: the fear that is being perpetuated as a result of the hatred we have for one another. It is as though this has become a social norm, and we have become immune to what is happening around us. If these issues continue to go unaddressed, it is only a matter of time before you and I become victims of these acts of hatred that are replaying themselves over and over on our television sets.

When I was growing up, my grandfather kept guns in our home, but as a child, I knew they were completely off-limits. Although my cousins and I played cops and robbers all the time, the thought of ever picking up a real gun NEVER crossed our minds. We knew that if our grandfather even thought that we were thinking about a gun the wrong way, his belt would be coming for us. More importantly, my grandparents always took the time to talk to all of us grandkids. I'm so thankful they showed their love for us and cared enough to be in our business. I am glad for every whipping I had because it helped guide my conscience toward righteousness when they were not around.

A few of the kids from our neighborhood come over to my home all the time to play. A lot of the time, I just sit back and observe. When I say to you that our youth generation is lost, I am not telling you what I heard; I am telling you what I know. Two of the kids from the neighborhood came over one Wednesday to see what I was doing. During their visit, they talked about how lucky my kids were to have a father like me. They went on to talk about how their mom was going out later that night, and my heart immediately went out to them as I sat there, now understanding what they meant by their compliments. As parents, we must do better! Our kids are oblivious to what this world is trying to do to them. They have no real guidance, so they turn to social media. They suffer from a lack of quality role models, so they are easily influenced. They are exposed to all that is wrong in the world, so it is hard for them to understand and discern what is right. We have failed our youth, but it is not too late.

Men, listen! If you want your kids to be better than you, play with them and teach them lessons at the same time. That's how they relate to us as adults through playing. Play their games with them and teach them little lessons like listening, respect, and honesty. I promise they will love you forever.

Talk to your kids more. Ask them about their day. Ask them what they are learning in school. Ask them about God. Get to know them more and spend time with them. You cannot tell me that what we see in our youth today is the way it is supposed to be. A lot of our youth turn to the streets or to their peers for guidance, leaving them to raise themselves or leaving them to raise other children. This leaves them lost with no one who has had any bona fide experience in life to lead them. Naturally, they start trying to figure things out on their own, which, in a lot of cases, leads them down the wrong paths very quickly. They then find themselves on the wrong side of the system, which was designed against minorities in the first place. Therefore, it is imperative that adults step up. The world we live in is dependent on us! People complain about what they see going on in the world but lack the effort to get involved. Even if you are not a parent, there are still kids who need you. If all you can do is just speak to them, sometimes that is enough.

The two most important relationships you can have is with God and yourself. My kids see me as the world, and that is all that matters. They know who I am, and no one can ever change that. My kids look up to me as an example, so I have no choice but to come through and live the words that I try to teach them daily. No man is perfect; thus, he will commit mistakes. It's up to us to examine those mistakes and learn from them. You cannot commit to the same patterns and think that the fabric will change. While a lot of our systems do need major reform, we cannot continue to place all the blame on a system when our generations are in the social/mental state that they are in. Take action into your own hands. Prevention resides within education. Don't allow a broken system or lack of protocol to be the excuse for our youth; they deserve better. We argued about standing for a flag, but how many of us will stand up for our youth?

Humanity, along with this world, have both been here a long time, and there are many lessons that are written in all spiritually inspired texts. The times which we live in have been written about long before you and I were on this earth. There are many lessons in the text, but the most important parts surround the concepts of Love, Truth, and righteousness. Love is patient, Love is kind. Truth is that which bears evidence of righteousness. In these days and times, there is an attack on all these things from all forms. You must recognize the truth of this world and keep in mind that many people turn to hate because the truth has become unpopular. We must never cease to seek these things, even when facing persecution from those who have self-proclaimed versions of them. Contrary to popular belief, there is but one way to Love, Truth and righteousness!

How much is enough? This world is passing away as we speak, and we continue to hate one another to the point of violence and even death. When will we realize that unity is the way, not division? Then again, most will not see this message, and only a few who see it will understand it. Change starts now. We may not have until tomorrow to start getting it together. There's only one true way, although many choose a different way.

READ
John 1:29
Ephesians 1:11-23
John 14:6
Revelations 13:7-10

A FIRE is kindled, and people are still debating over a wall, but Ezekiel provides a valuable lesson to those who listened to the trumpets that went throughout the land just before The Day of The Lord. Remember, He is God Almighty, Lord of Heaven's Armies, and He is the only One that can save you, not your big, beautiful walls and definitely not those false lips you put your trust in! Choose LOVE and receive your covering of His Salvation in these days to come, or choose to allow hatred and division to trap you behind the walls of death. It's your choice!

One must not dwell on his mistakes but learn to avoid committing them over and over, expecting a different result.

READ
Ezekiel 13:10-15
Revelations 4:11

I may be poor by this world's standards, but I am rich in LOVE.

"**GREATNESS.**" A term many strive to achieve, but few people reach. True greatness comes through glorifying The One who created greatness! If we were created in His Greatness (**Genesis 1:27**), why does society give us the ideals that greatness is achieved by other means? Why are so many who think they have achieved greatness still struggling with things like depression, loneliness, lack of peace, selfishness, etc.? Greatness comes when we learn to Glorify the Creator of greatness. This is a call to be different from those who edify their existence through this world's view. When you base your existence on the world's view, you become subject to the world's problems. Thus, your greatness begins to conform merely to world standards.

Greatness is achieved through the actions that glorify The Giver of Greatness. Glory assigns meaning to life and everything you do! You were created to be greater than the world around you. If you seek to glorify the world around you, you will be disappointed in your works. However, if you seek to bring glory to Him who created the world and all things in it, you will rise above the world's standard and see the true greatness He created you to achieve.

READ
Colossians 1:9-11
Genesis 1:31
Isaiah 43:7
John 5:44

Praise the Creator, rebuke the adversary.
Be Different, Be Great.

CHAPTER VIII

REVELATION OF THE TIMES

*"The heavens declare the glory of God;
the skies proclaim the work of his hands."*
(Psalm 19:1, NIV)

CHAPTER 8
Revelation of The Times

Nowadays, our minds are so enslaved to this world that even when our vision is clear on the things that are going on, we struggle with believing in what is true. The truth has become a lie, and a lie has become the truth. Up is now down, and down is now up. Everyone is full of confusion, so much so that each chooses his own path along with his own truths. In these times, if you do not like the way you look, you can go to the local beauty shops and buy a new appearance. The beauty industry is at an all-time level of prosperity. If your hair is not long enough, you can go buy a sew-in. If your lashes are not long enough, just get extensions. If your lips are not full enough, get injections. If you are going bald or your hair is thinning out, just get an implant.

The truth is no longer considered to be true. A lie is made to be the truth, and the truth has become the lie. The man has become the woman, and the woman has become the man. Love is now hated, and hatred is now loved. The ways of the world have corrupted the minds of the people to the point that people are starting to believe that they are The Creator themselves and have taken the choice of life into their own hands. The wealth disparities are at an all-time high.

In an article published in December 2014, Pew Research noted that the "wealth gap between middle-income and upper-income families is widest on record," based on studies conducted from 1983 to 2013 (Pew Research Center, "America's Wealth Gap Between Middle-Income and Upper-Income Families Is Widest on Record," 2014). In a later article published in November 2017, they noted, "wealth gaps between upper-income families and lower- and middle-income families are at the highest levels recorded." This study, conducted from 2007 to 2016, concluded that the gaps had risen from 40% in 2007 to 75% in 2016 for upper-to-lower-income families (Pew Research Center, "How Wealth Inequality Has Changed in the U.S. Since the Great Recession, by Race, Ethnicity, and Income," 2017).

With that being said, the rich are richer than they have ever been, while the poor are getting poorer. The greed for money has become so widespread that brother will kill brother just to get ahead of one another. Families are ripped and torn apart after the death of a loved one, not out of grief but out of the wealth left behind by the deceased. Do not sell your soul to buy the attention of this world. You are a precious gem among rocks. Image is great, but it is even better to invest in your soul. Images fade or change with time, but the soul lasts forever. When the soul is beautiful on the inside, an outward glow becomes the result.

Even the heavens proclaim their signs in an ever-changing world, just as it is written. One thing that will never change, though, is the sovereignty of El Shaddai! His word is forever lasting, aboding in Truth, and He told us a long time ago about the things that are happening now and the things that are to come. How long will we continue to enslave ourselves to this moribund world and ignore Him?

Read
1 John 2:15-17
1 Corinthians 7:31
Psalms 19:1, 89:11, 97:6

What information/influences are you allowing to instruct you? Truth is the way! The truth causes those who love the lie to become discombobulated. I'm learning this more and more each day and allowing His words to light my path. I have been on the wrong path for sooo long, riding solo and not giving Glory to Yahweh! The road to being God-led may be long, but He will never fail, so who am I to think I can go at it alone and not put you as my number one light? Glory to the True Creator for being with me in the beginning, throughout, and forever! Thank You for taking me to low places so that I would Lift You up above all things!

READ
Isaiah 10:4-34, 11:11-16

If your brain is not in learning mode, then you are going nowhere. Elevate your mind and release it from the mental prisons designed to keep you from thinking on your own! Look at what is going on in this world. Wake up! Either you are for God, or you are against Him; there is no in-between! Will you rise above or be stuck below? If today was the only day of the week that you celebrated the Goodness of God by picking up His word, you are doing it all wrong. The good news is that if you receive the gift of grace tomorrow, you can start there with the blessings of a brand-new day that you have never seen before. One day a week is not what being close to God is. If you say you know God and you claim that you are a child of the Most High, one or two days out of the week will not keep you within the Kingdom of Heaven.

If you have opened your eyes each morning all week long, this means God has been with you all your days; thus, you should be able to spend at least five uninterrupted minutes with Him daily. You claim to be a Christian, Muslim, Jew, Hindu, Rastafarian, Buddhist, Sikh, etc., but your life is too busy to spend time with what you believe in until something bad happens. Start with five uninterrupted minutes by letting His Words speak to you. Begin with the question, "Where are You, God?" Ask Him for His understanding, and then apply that understanding to your life each day you get from that point forward. Remove the mediocrity in your life and come into the growth He has in store for you. Allow peace to come into your life, and truly understand the gift that a new day brings to your purpose.

Intellectuals transcend the boundaries that have been placed around them. In real life, there are no boundaries other than the limits you place on yourself. Don't be afraid to live outside of what you have been taught all your life. That is not living for you, that is existing by the constraints placed around us by others. All you have to do is have faith, believe and trust in yourself, make better choices, and have a little patience. The blessings will come. You are the key to unlocking the happiness you want out of life.

I have a plan for YOU, but do you trust in God?

Those who live for the moment and only look out for themselves are selfish at best. They will do anything at a moment's notice, live by the seat of their pants, and do anything for money. Remember, you cannot take money or fame with you when you leave this realm. God is the way, not these worldly things.

READ
Psalms 49:5-20

Hatred in your heart = Destruction within your spirit

CHAPTER IX

WHAT WOULD YOU DO FOR ETERNITY?

"And even the very hairs of your head are all numbered."
(Matthew 10:30, NIV)

CHAPTER 9
What Would You Do for Eternity?

What would you do for eternity? The answer to that question requires you to think about eternity, but most of us cannot even think for a second. Why? Because it requires that you see things differently, act differently, and focus differently. It would also require your path to be completely different than it has been in the past. Would your walk be different if your thoughts were for eternity and not just for a lifetime? Imagine if a second becomes more like a minute, a minute becomes an hour, an hour becomes a day, and a day is now a year. How important would every single choice made become? Again, this would require that your actions moving forward be different from what they were when your thoughts were only focused on a lifetime. Naturally, your focus would not be on you as much as it is when you think within the constraints of the paradox of a lifespan. It would require you to eliminate your focus on meaningless things that are constantly passing away. What if I told you that this could be achieved, but it would require you to empty yourself of your current thoughts, focuses, and actions?

Eternity is what you gain with The Creator, and with Him, a day is like a year. The smallest of details can change the biggest outcome, but it requires focus on eternity to reach this desired outcome. It is in the details that our Creator is concerned, so much so that He knows every single hair on our bodies and every single tear that you have shed. The choices we make going forward would require more focus on the details. The past is set in stone and there is nothing we can do to change that which has already taken place. Our hope then should be fixed on what we can change. Change starts today! Your beginning does not have to be your ending, but now is the time. What will you do differently to live out those things that are of eternal life?

READ
Matthew 10:30

Wired at a higher current, you could not handle this voltage.

Most people are so scared of failure that they become cautious about every aspect of their lives, yet they have the audacity to wonder why they never see success. All success is the byproduct of failure, and it comes when you learn to subtract fear.

You must get comfortable with being uncomfortable in order to grow.

We are living in the times that have been written about for many years now. In an age where each has turned to his own ways, forgotten about LOVE and compassion, and lost faith in The One who delivered us here. We have turned from the purpose of existence in this precious amount of time that we have here, and we have turned towards the ways of the earth. Earth is not our final resting place! We were not meant to remain on this planet forever, only for a period of time! If it were so, why is it guaranteed that mankind will experience death at least once? What man lives forever and does not age over time? What woman's beauty does not fade with each turn of a new moon? Time is forever pressing onward and while we have it, we should be careful with how we use it while we are here.

READ
Acts 14:15-17
Hebrews 13:14

While we are here, we ought to be able to be thankful for each second we are allowed to take a breath of air into our nostrils. This is confirmation that you and I have been awarded a gift from The Almighty Gift Giver. These gifts, which I am referring to, are the gifts of Mercy and Grace. Grace, what is it? Some define grace as courteous goodwill, while others say it is to bring honor or credit to someone or something, and many call it favor. To be in it (Grace) implies that you had to receive it, and to receive it is to be in the presence of The Most High. The Most High is purposeful in His ways. To receive favor in His eyes is to know that He has not given up on your ability to fulfill His purpose in your life. It is not until this purpose has been fulfilled that we are delivered back to judgment, where we are given the opportunity to be delivered to Glory. We all must leave this world one day. What type of legacy will you leave behind? If you do not like the answer, it is time for a change. The clock is ticking!

From God, we are all given; to Him, we must all return.

Glory is to be given to The Purpose Giver over our lives, so while we are afforded the gift of time, what will you do to seek out His purpose over your life? Someone was not afforded this gift that you have today, as they are no longer here to live on this borrowed time. Although you may still have it, what are you going to do with it before you must give it back? Remember, life has a funny way of humbling those who are proud at heart.

I know because I was once that very person, running the world without knowledge or care for My Creator. Thankfully, He saw me in all my foolishness and still kept me safe. Even when all of my lies were catching up to me, He never left my side. In my moments of trouble, He looked at me and said, "I have a bigger plan for you!"

As I look back on those times, I am grateful He was able to turn me around and allow me to return to Him so that I could receive His Mercy and Grace. When life happens, remember that you, too, can lean on Him, and He is there for you! Forgive yourself, come humbly to Him full of truth, and see how He renews your Heart and Spirit!

CHAPTER X

THE RACE FOR HUMANITY

"He also said, 'This is what the kingdom of God is like. A man scatters seed on the ground.'" (Mark 4:26, NIV)

CHAPTER 10
The Race for Humanity

I will open this closing chapter with a short poem I wrote titled: ***Our Will vs His Will***

Our will is often spoken a ton,
but rarely is it ever acted upon.
It is often talked about,
But almost always intertwined with doubt.
Pushed like a rhetorical question,
expecting change like the flip of the pages.
failing to realize the entire time,
that our will and His Will were on two dissimilar stages.

So, why have I taken the time to bring you these thoughts? The answer is simple: I hope that the words of this book will bring you one step closer to the promise so many have fallen short of in our lifetime. Life is a journey full of many moments, some good and some bad. We only get one life, and there is no easy path to the greatness we were all created to achieve. Many stumble through it with the impression that this is all that we get. Life is merely a test! I would say that it is a test of endurance and one that is designed to bring all into the perfectness of the joys of LOVE.

LOVE, what is it? Love endures through all things. LOVE is not selfish, and it does not imply that hurt will not be experienced in it. On the contrary, those who LOVE the most experience many trials and tribulations in order to shape them into the perfectness of LOVE. Without shaping, we become self-evident, self-aware, self-centered, and downright selfish.

Mankind's heart was set on evil from the moment the enemy of our Greatness was cast out of the place of peace. The enemy's plan has been to keep those with any ounce of LOVE in their hearts from seeing and receiving the LOVE that The Creator of all beings has for us. He knows what it is like to be in the presence of the Beneficent, but he knows that his evil ways have prevented him from ever getting back to that Glory that is promised to all those who choose to do the righteous works.

Works, what are these works that are spoken of? Works come through understanding the Will of The Most High. In order to understand the Will, you must read. Therefore, I have encouraged you throughout the reading of this work to reference various scriptures. I want you to keep in mind that all the passages have additional context before and after them. To assign the meaning that was intended by the writer, you need to read the full content. You should also be encouraged, though. The understanding you seek lies within The Word.

Reading the works inspired by the Prophets sent before us will lead to the understanding that you so desperately desire. It will open you up to what we see going on in the times that we are in right now, which were prophesied about well before this age. Seek knowledge and understanding from Him. He will guide you to the wisdom of the likeness of a child's mind. This wisdom will lead you to fulfilling the actions of the knowledge and understanding you get from the reading you have done. Change will come knocking at your front door, but make sure that you are ready to receive it. This does not mean that you will not experience trouble, but remember, He does not trust everyone with trouble just to leave them. As a refiner cuts a precious stone to bring it into near-perfect luster, so will your problems shape you into Light and Truth.

If someone told you that you were created in the image of the Creator to be a reflection of God and that every decision you made from this point on reflected that image, how would it change your decisions going forward? The truth is this: we, mankind, were all created in the image of God and in His likeness (**Genesis 1:27**). Since we were created in His image and likeness, we should be able to see this same image in others and treat them as you would like for them to treat you (**Luke 6:31**). None of us had the opportunity of choosing the image our eyes see when we look at one another, so why is it that we are so quick to judge each other based on appearances?

What we see is merely a shell, a vessel in which our souls dwell. The soul is what we ought to be seeking in others instead of forming judgment based on the exterior appearance. It is this very judgment, which we are all guilty of, that will be the same judgment rendered to us if we cannot learn to overcome it (**Matthew 7:1-2**). From the moment we get the call to be sent into the world by being born into time on this earth, the world begins its works on us. The choice to be sent into time was predetermined by the Creator. Who will withstand the test of time? No one knows how long they have in this fleshly vessel before they will be called to their resting place, so why live as though you belong to a part of this world?

World-wide disasters are becoming increasingly common today. At every turn, there is a new form of hate or a new form of division. Our systems are designed by people who are supposed to be designing them with the purpose of helping the very people whom they were elected to represent. All the while, these systems are oppressing those very same people. The rich are getting richer at the expense of the poor. The truth is being called a lie, and the lie is being widely accepted as the truth.

Even the Declaration of Independence declares, "We hold these truths to be self-evident, that all Men are created equal, that they are endowed by their Creator with certain unalienable Rights, that among these are Life, Liberty, and the Pursuit of Happiness" (Jefferson, US 1776), yet, the choice is made to separate families as though they are animals.

What is the truth? We are on the brink of a harvest. These times were supposed to happen, according to what was written many years before these times. These divisions are necessary in order for you to be able to clearly see the children of God and those who do the works of the enemy. If it had not been this way, it would have been hard for you to spot the weeds amongst the good grain. Good grain will be separated at the end of time, just as a sifter who sifts flour. The grain will be identified by the works, just as weeds will be spotted in a like manner.

If the harvest were today, would you be confident about the pile you ended up in? If your answer is no, it is time to change your work. If you are reading these words, the good news is that you have been given another opportunity. The grace and mercy that you received today should be used to look in the mirror.

Start there because the mirror will reveal the truth about who you really are. It may be scary, but do not turn away. Accept what you see and commit to changing it while you still have a chance to do so. Ask for His forgiveness and prepare yourself to Step By Faith. See yourself in all who you encounter and challenge yourself to treat them how you would want to be treated.

READ
1 Corinthians 9:10-11
Mark 4:26-33

John 4:34-38
Job 4:8
Matthew 9:37-38
James 3:18
Galatians 6:8-10

This life is merely preparation for our destination.

The worker was sent forth to prepare the field. It was almost ripe and ready for harvest. This was yet the beginning. Afterward, the harvest was made, and the good crop was separated from the bad crop. Each crop was awarded based on its character. The good crop was used to glorify the Planter. The bad crop was thrown back into the field to later be burned with the useless stock.

READ
Revelations 14:14-20

Oh, my dear brothers and sisters, how I longed for you to be able to escape the traps of the enemy that were set to entangle you. Can't you see what is going on in the world around you? Have the signs of the Times not been revealed to you? When will enough suffering be enough? Sin is sin, regardless of how mankind chooses to punish it. No sin is greater than any other sin, as they ALL lead to the same destination, and the wage of sin is death. Let the first person without sin be the one to judge another for their sins. So, to say that mankind should come up with these types of laws when all mankind has sinned is like saying we should cut out the tongues of the person who lies.

The enemy's plan was set in motion long before you and me. Can't you recognize it? The hatred, envy, and greed that so many have experienced is just a small part of it. Look around you; the divisions are at an all-time high, the value of human life is no longer precious, and lies are widely accepted as the truth. The enemy laid his trap, but The Truth will always shine its light on the very ground the enemy laid the trap on! All Praises be to The Creator for Him allowing the victory over those who set their traps! He sent His anointed One to show us the way and to provide salvation to those who wholeheartedly believe and to write their name in the books of eternity. Thank you for revealing them and for keeping account of their actions, as all are called to accountability in the end!

This is not the way! This is not righteousness! Yet so many of us have fallen victim to these very agendas the enemy wanted us to fall for. People of God, wake up and see the signs of the world around you! Even the earth is showing us the signs of what is to come, and you cannot tell me that you have not seen it with your own eyes. Fix it now! Find truth, seek wisdom, and show love. These are the only things that will last in these trying times we are in, not your wealth. It is greed that has led to these things that are going on, but love is the only gift you are going to be able to take with you in the end of days.

The very kingdom of Heaven is upon our doorsteps, yet so many have chosen to walk through the gates of hell! Wake up and look around you. Even the heavens are declaring the handiwork of All Mighty God Himself! Time is passing by right before our eyes. All will have to give an account of what we chose to do with the time that was given to us. The thing about time is the fact that it is so precious. We often waste it on the most meaningless things, thinking that we have a ton of it.

The Reality is that it is only when it is too late that we realize how valuable it is. It is time to start eliminating wasted time and start maximizing it by focusing on what really matters.

    Famines, earthquakes, pestilence, floods, wildfires, volcanoes erupting, and rumors of war, just to name a few of the signs of the times, yet mankind is still deaf, blind, and ignorant of what is in front of their very faces! All-time record high temperatures are happening worldwide. Water shortages are happening in places that historically were known to have an abundance of resources. People these days are calling themselves "The Messiah," yet their mouths speak words of division, and their actions are those of hatred. Humans are leaving this world in droves. These are the times that have been written about! The prophets did not come in times of peace and righteousness. They came on the contrary, but very few heeded their warnings. I'm thankful for the opportunity to repent of those things which I have done against Your Will. I will sing praises to Your Name until the end of time as we may know it! May peace be upon the oppressed and poor from the Light Shiner who is exalted Above!

READ
Psalms 69:21-36
Psalms 22:19-23
Proverbs 31:6-31
Mark 15:22-24
Isaiah 53:12

    This is a wake-up call for those who have been sleeping. Turn now while He is still giving out time! I know that not everyone will like my words today, but this message is not meant to tickle and massage your ears as a lie would. It is meant for you to understand that The One who allowed you to read this message sent signs to this world that you may pay heed to Him! So, I plead with you all, find love and act on it, read His word, and bring it into existence while we still have the time to do so!

It is written,

"A brother will betray his brother to death, a father will betray his own child, and children will rebel against their parents and cause them to be killed." Matthew 10:21.

"And everyone will hate you because you are my followers. But the one who endures to the end will be saved." - Matthew 10:22.

"The day is coming when you will see the sacrilegious object that causes desecration standing where he should not be." (Reader, pay attention!) Then, those in Judea must flee to the hills. Mark 13:14.

Look around you! It is evident what is happening! The encouragement that I bring you is as follows: after every major loss, there came an abundance to those who could withstand the tests of time. This is one of His many promises:

The LORD says, *"I will rescue those who love me. I will protect those who trust in my name. When they call on me, I will answer; I will be with them in trouble. I will rescue and honor them. I will reward them with a long life and give them my salvation."* (Psalms 91:14-16, New Living Translation, Tyndale House Publishers, 1996, 2004, 2007, 2015)

READ
Hebrew 12:26-29
2 Peter 1
Romans 15
Acts 2:38-40

In Closing, I first must give an Honor to The Lord Most High for sending a Savior into this world so that we would all have an example of His LOVE for all of us. It is through Him that I have been able to bring you these words. Without Him, I am nothing, so I am forever grateful. He looked past all my years of trying to figure it out on my own, and He did a new thing for me. To Him, I give all the Glory! Hallelujah, Jehovah Jireh!! Alhamdulillah! He alone is My Rock and Savior. He gives us but one life that we would be able to survive the test of time and become perfected in His Love through all things. Just as a rough stone must be cut and polished, I hope that this book has provided you with a little more shaping toward the ultimate goals of LOVE and peace.

PHOTOGRAPHY BY THE AUTHOR

THE TRUTH ABOUT THE WEALTH OF GOD'S LOVE

Tepotzotlan, México 2

The Mount of Olives, David, Jerusalem

Garden of Gethsemane, Jerusalem

Teotihuacán, México

Zócalo, México City

Emirates Palace, Abu Dhabi

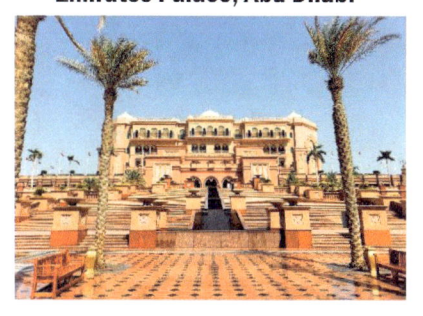

Sheikh Zayed Grand Mosque, Abu Dhabi

Taal Volcano, Philippines

Makati, Philippines

Temppeliaukion Church, Helsinki

Taj Mahal Agra, India

Cristo De Redentor, Brazil

Uspenski Cathedral, Finland

Amsterdam, Netherlands

The Jordan River, Israel

Mount Carmel, Jaffa Israel

The Sea of Galilee, Israel

Jericho, Israel

Eiffel Tower, Paris

Notre Dame, Paris

Louvre Museum, Paris

ACCORDING TO THE TEXT

Bible References

ACCORDING TO THE TEXT
Bible References

I: WHAT IS LOVE?
- Ephesians 4:32
- John 3:16
- 1 John 4:7-21

II: PEOPLE AND THEIR IMPACT ON YOUR LIFE
- Job 1:6, 2:1
- 1 John 3:7-10
- James 1:15, 2:19, 3:15
- Ephesians 2:1-10
- Psalms 14:1-6
- John 14:6, 15:1-17
- Romans 2:4
- 1 Peter 2:20
- Hebrews 12:25-29
- 2 Peter 2:10-22
- Matthew 23:11-12
- Luke 22:26
- Mark 10:43-45
- James 1:23-25
- Exodus 14:14
- Isaiah 49:25

- Psalms 35:1, 109:3
- Proverbs 15:18, 20:3
- 2 Timothy 2:23

III: "THE CHANGE YOU ARE CALLING FOR STARTS WITH US"
- James 1:26-27
- James 2:1-12
- James 3:13-18
- James 4:1-10
- 2 Samuel 9

IV: NOT ALLOWING THE PAST TO CONTROL YOUR FUTURE
- Genesis 1:26-27
- Deuteronomy 20:3-4
- Numbers 20:10-12
- Deuteronomy 31:1-2
- Proverbs 16:3-4

MINI STORIES
- Matthew 17:20, 21:21-22
- Hebrews 11
- James 4:12
- Judges 18:1-6
- Micah 7:7
- Romans 5:3-11
- Colossians 1:9-14

- Galatians 6:7-10
- Genesis 1:31, 3:1-19
- James 1:19-27, 4:1-10
- Genesis 17:1-8,48
- Jeremiah 31:1-14

VII: THE WORLD WE LIVE IN TODAY
- John 1:29
- Ephesians 1:11-23
- John 14:6
- Revelations 13:7-10
- Ezekiel 13:10-15
- Revelations 4:11
- Colossians 1:9-11
- Genesis 1:31
- Isaiah 43:7
- John 5:44

VIII: REVELATION OF THE TIMES
- 1 John 2:15-17
- 1 Corinthians 7:31
- Psalms 19:1, 89:11, 97:6
- Isaiah 10:4-34, 11:11-16
- Psalms 49:5-20

IX: WHAT WOULD YOU DO FOR ETERNITY?
- Matthew 10:30
- Acts 14:15-17
- Hebrews 13:14

X: THE RACE FOR HUMANITY
- 1 Corinthians 9:10-11
- Mark 4:26-33
- John 4:34-38
- Job 4:8
- Matthew 9:37-38
- James 3:18
- Galatians 6:8-10
- Revelations 14:14-20
- Psalms 69:21-36
- Psalms 22:19-23
- Proverbs 31:6-31
- Mark 15:22-24
- Isaiah 53:12
- Hebrew 12:26-29
- 2 Peter 1
- Romans 15
- Acts 2:38-40

FROM POVERTY TO PROSPERITY
THE TRUTH ABOUT THE WEALTH OF GOD'S LOVE

ABOUT THE AUTHOR

ABOUT THE AUTHOR
NIKIA ANDERSON

Contact

Website: www.obfconline.com
Email: AnOverstandingWord@gmail.com

Social Media

Instagram: @Nikia.media
YouTube: www.YouTube.com/Nikia17

ABOUT THE AUTHOR

Nikia Anderson is an American self-published author from Nashville, Arkansas. He was born to Donna Anderson and Darrell McFadden in Hope, Arkansas, on January 18, 1984. Poverty was a huge part of his early childhood, as he did not have running water until around the age of 7. At an early age, Nikia was intrigued by building things with his hands, which led to his excelling academically in school. Being an honor student all the way through middle school, Nikia decided to try sports. Football became his dominant sport moving into high school, earning him several sports awards and scholarships. Nikia graduated from Nashville High School with Honors in 2002. He turned down his athletic scholarships to attend the University of Arkansas at Little Rock under an academic scholarship. He pursued a degree in Computer Science, although he did not graduate.

Later in life, he would enter the Learning and Development field as a Trainer. This career afforded him the opportunity to travel around the world, leading him to eventually write about his life journey and experiences. He started the website StepByFaith.com and became the first self-published author in his family on September 26, 2019. As the 2020 pandemic temporarily ended most of his international travel, he turned to local attractions within his new home state of Arizona. After experiencing a historic and unprecedented year in Social Justice, Nikia decided it was time for him to give power to his voice by studying the extensive works of those before him and educating himself on various historical events that led up to the movements that swept the world in 2020.

It was on this precipice that the ideology of "The Modern-Day Slave" came to the forefront of his second literary work. He would title it as such, coining the words that he used to describe what he calls the mental yoke of bondage by the modern-day enemy to The Creator of mankind. In this book, Nikia explored the full history of physical slavery, not just from a Western viewpoint of the Transatlantic Slave Trade narrative but from a more holistic and ancient civilization standpoint. Once he arrived at the point of the abolition of most forms of physical slavery by the 19th century, he explored the economic, sociological, and psychological impacts that physical slavery has on our world today. One troubling example that Nikia helped his readers to understand was the touchy subject of Racism and the impacts of its introduction into our societies. He focused on what we must do in order to arrive at a place of human unity, justice, and equity for all through purposeful re-education of the human being.

References

Jefferson, T. (US 1776). *The Declaration of Independence.* Retrieved from https://etc.usf.edu/lit2go/133/historic-american-documents/4957/the-declaration-of-independence/

Noor Foundation International, I. (2018). *The Holy Qur'an 13th Reprint.* Hockessin, DE 19707: Noor Foundation International, Inc.

Pew Research Center, W. D. (2014, December 17). *America's wealth gap between middle-income and upper-income families is widest on record.* Retrieved from Pew Research Center: https://www.pewresearch.org/fact-tank/2014/12/17/wealth-gap-upper-middle-income/

Pew Research Center, W. D. (2017, November 1). *How wealth inequality has changed in the U.S. since the Great Recession, by race, ethnicity and income.* Retrieved from Pewresearch.org: https://www.pewresearch.org/fact-tank/2017/11/01/how-wealth-inequality-has-changed-in-the-u-s-since-the-great-recession-by-race-ethnicity-and-income/

Tyndale House Foundation. (1996, 2004, 2007, 2015). *Holy Bible, New Living Translation.* Carol Stream, Illinois 60188: Tyndale House Publishers, Inc.

Made in the USA
Columbia, SC
08 February 2025